Birth
to
Five

Edward Short

Foreword by Lord Annan, OBE

PITMAN PUBLISHING

First published 1974

Sir Isaac Pitman and Sons Ltd
Pitman House, Parker Street, Kingsway, London WC2B 5PB
P.O. Box 46038, Banda Street, Nairobi, Kenya

Sir Isaac Pitman (Aust.) Pty Ltd
Pitman House, 158 Bouverie Street, Carlton, Victoria 3053, Australia

Pitman Publishing Corporation
6 East 43rd Street, New York, NY 10017, USA

Sir Isaac Pitman (Canada) Ltd
495 Wellington Street West, Toronto 135, Canada

The Copp Clark Publishing Company
517 Wellington Street West, Toronto 135, Canada

ISBN: 0 273 31865 9

Text set in 11/12 pt. Photon Times, printed by photolithography,
and bound in Great Britain at The Pitman Press, Bath
G4682:15

Foreword

When Plato asked in *The Republic* how justice was to be established in the State he ended by discussing education; and ever since Plato's day education has seemed to be one of the means open to men to make the world they live in better.

In the past people thought this could be done by extending education forward. Universal primary education led to the extension of the school-leaving age and secondary education created the demand for a variety of institutions for higher and further education. But Ted Short is advocating an extension backwards. And with good reason. The more we study the intractable and damnable problem of poverty, the more it becomes apparent that the chances of a child born of poor parents lifting himself out of his milieu by his ability are still almost as remote as they ever were. Despite the improvement in primary schools, despite the attempt to postpone as late as possible—and certainly later than eleven plus—an irrevocable decision regarding a child's future, despite the new methods of teaching and vastly increased expenditure, the truth is that educational opportunities cannot on their own counteract the effects of blinding inequality.

To-day half a million children will be born of parents so poor that their mothers will have had inadequate protein during pregnancy. They will grow up under-nourished and they will perform badly at school. Families in multiple deprivation areas stagger under multiple handicaps because everything in the area in which they live—from housing to libraries—will be sub-standard. We have come to realize that the disadvantages from which all children of less well-educated families suffer can hardly be eliminated during their time at school. To picture them catching up in an imaginary race is an illusion; they start too far behind.

This is the problem Ted Short discusses in this book, and he comes up with one answer to this multiple question problem. The nursery school.

If we want to do something to enable children to perform better at school, we must start to help them before they go there. In the nursery school children get for a few hours a day those contacts with other children, that adult attention which they need and may not get at home. A palliative? All social reforms are palliatives. There is no one all-embracing plan which, if we could discover and implement, would solve the ills of our society. But the nursery school is one necessary step forward if we are to diminish inequality.

NOEL ANNAN

Preface

Our schools have always had to give a disproportionate amount of their time to remedial teaching because the simple fact is that by the time children enter the Infant School they are set in their ways to a remarkable degree. The foundations of personality, language, attitudes, values, basic skills, as well as the capacity for intellectual development, are all laid—for good or ill—and can only be changed with considerable difficulty.

The pre-school years are the magic years when the helpless new-born baby grows into an active, sturdy, well-established little person. Never again in his whole life-span will his brain, his personality or his skills develop so rapidly, so much, or so fundamentally. Never again will his environment, no matter how sophisticated it may become later in life with its people, its things, its sounds, its smells, its spaces, influence him so profoundly. It is a terrifying thought, but there is now agreement that by and large the five-year-old has become the person he will always be. The foundations are completed and will to a considerable extent dictate the nature of the building.

Now, of course, if all parents were intelligent, affectionate, articulate people, if no mothers were in full-time employment, if all families were of reasonable size, and if all homes were spacious, light friendly places with lots of objects of the kind and shape which evoke the great magician in every child, there would be little to worry about. But of course they are not.

The sheer economics of keeping up with the Joneses or, indeed, of making ends meet has made the working mother the rule rather than the exception in both working-class and middle-class homes. Because of the shortage of nursery places in maintained schools this development has necessarily led to a considerable growth of private-enterprise child-care. This ranges from the playgroup run, and well run, by volunteer mums, to the rather squalid and often illegal back-street child-minder to be found in any of our large towns.

In recent years a great volume of research has revealed another shadow across large numbers of our children—a shadow from which many never emerge. The correlation between social, economic and cultural deprivation and depressed educational attainment is now incontrovertible. Equally impressive is the evidence that the retardation appears, and indeed is quantifiable, before school age, that it is cumulative and that remedial action becomes more difficult the longer it is delayed. Eventually, and at a quite early age, it becomes virtually impossible. It follows from this that compensatory educational effort is most effective in the pre-school years and least effective, often impossible, in the secondary school.

Our failure to recognize this in the provision of nursery education for all mothers who need it for their children must be responsible for a colossal waste of resources in the primary and secondary schools seen not only in the extent of remedial teaching, which probably absorbs one-tenth of our total teaching capacity, but also in the army of young people who leave school without coming near to raising their attainment to the level of their potential.

It is indefensible to ignore all we have learnt about young children and about deprivation in the past quarter century in planning our education system and allocating resources within it. This book makes this point, describes what is being done in the voluntary and local authority provision of pre-school education, and how more can and should be done, and done quickly, to meet the need.

Michael is the author's son.

Acknowledgements

The photographs in this book were taken in the Ravenswood Infant School, Newcastle-upon-Tyne, and are reproduced by courtesy of Newcastle-upon-Tyne's *Civic News*.

Contents

1. Birth to Five

The pre-school child is, by definition, outside the statutory period of school life but he is, nevertheless, our major educational problem at the present time. There are two reasons for this. First, we know with much more certainty than in the past that the early years are the most formative years, the years in which both education and deprivation can make their optimum and most lasting impact. Secondly, social habits are changing. Housework, which only a generation ago was a full-time occupation for the mother, has been transformed by mechanization and by better planning and design. This and the attractions of a higher family income have led to many, probably a majority, of mothers doing full-time or part-time work outside the home.

These two factors, added to the widespread interest in education which is not by any means confined to one social class, and the much greater expectations of it, have given rise to a nation-wide demand for nursery education which has been seen in recent years in the remarkable growth of the playgroup movement, which now involves 200,000 children throughout the country, as well as in the Nursery School Association petition in 1972. The demand has come from all classes, sometimes to release the mother to work, but much more often because of a well-informed belief that it can provide a valuable supplement to the educational influence of the home or compensate for it where it is inadequate. In a survey carried out in 1971 in a working-class area of Newcastle-upon-Tyne 78 per cent of mothers thought a child who had been to nursery school had an advantage over children who had not.[1] (See page 65.)

Nothing less than pre-school education for all parents who want it is

---

[1] Superior numerals in the text refer to the identifying numbers in the list of References on pages 125–6.

demanded. This presents central government, local government and the teaching profession with a considerable problem and challenge—by far the biggest physical and educational problem in the education service in the present decade.

The starting point of the educational problem is an understanding of the pre-school child, for his needs arise from the way in which he grows—intellectually and emotionally as well as physically—and education is concerned with all three. And his needs cannot be met until the pattern of his growth and development is known and understood.

The normal nursery education period from three to five is a segment, a tremendously important segment, in a process of growth which is continuous from conception to the early twenties. The mother has been an active partner in a dialogue of growth and affection. She grows in a very real sense with her child. She was there at the start and she has seen and been involved in it all. Her empathy and identification with her child is by far the strongest example of attachment between human beings. Up to three she has probably never been parted from him for more than a few hours—and maybe not even that. She has an acute sense of a process of continuous growth. She may record and recall with pride the emergence of every glimmer of understanding, every rudimentary skill. The detailed record of Michael's development mentioned throughout this chapter is an example of maternal understanding of, and interest in, the process of child development.

The nursery-school teacher and the playgroup leader on the other hand lack the mother's instinctive and functional advantage, although of course they may be parents themselves. In normal circumstances they take in a sturdy, confident, well-established child aged three. Not unnaturally they tend to regard him at that point in his development as the base-line for all the care they will lavish on him. Of course they are not alone in this. All teachers have to struggle against the temptation—the infant teacher who gets her pupils at five, the primary teacher at seven and their secondary colleague at eleven. All are tempted to forget that three, five, seven and eleven have no special nodality inherent in them, but are merely points on the moving escalator of growth and development—originally decided upon almost accidentally as products of the availability of buildings and teachers as the education system was created.

The teacher of young children continually has to remind herself of this—and mere reminding is not sufficient; she must almost become obsessed with the key concept of continuous growth. Her task is to put herself in the mother's place, truly *in loco parentis*—or, if she is wise, *cum parente*. That is what nursery education is all about. But if she is to begin to compensate for her inevitable handicap *vis-à-vis* the mother she should understand the norms and sequence of development in the years before her children come to her. If she fails to acquire this knowledge she can never begin to understand the individual patterns of development of her own children. And their development may be as unique as their faces.

It is also important for mothers to remember another related truth. The child's life and his vulnerability to environment begin with conception and not with birth—indeed the most profound and lasting environmental influence can probably take place in the last few months of pregnancy. During the first three months, the most rapid period of growth in his life-cycle, the unicellular creature develops into a multicellular one, re-enacting the great cosmic drama of Genesis. Amoeba to mammal. Meanwhile the child lives in the deeply peaceful world of the womb, suspended in fluid which isolates him from gravity, temperature change, light and probably sound, except his mother's heart-beat. Yet in spite of the peace and protection which envelop him, he may be at risk.

There is considerable and growing evidence that the child's development, physical, intellectual and emotional, is not merely the product of his genetic inheritance and his post-natal environment, but that the gestational period is also of major importance in determining development. The effect of nutritional and other deprivation is discussed in Chapter 4.

Birth itself is an event, sometimes an extremely traumatic one, but still only an incident without much significance in the life-cycle. The most dramatic and rapid growth of bodily tissues takes place during pregnancy and in the few months after birth. There is then a swift fall in the rate of growth in the first two or three years and a slower fall after the age of three. At birth the baby is mauled for the first time. Gravity, temperature and sound all immediately assail him. However much he may search for Shangri-la in later life he will never regain the deep peace of the womb. However strong the symbiosis of mother and child may be, it can never be quite the same again. But in the immediate post-birth period the mother by her care, protection, closeness and cuddling will try to make her child's existence approximate as closely as possible to his pre-birth life. Of course she will not be a person to him, but a vague, warm, nourishing something which envelops him and eases the transition from womb to outside world. This is his birthright, and if he is denied it his unfolding personality may suffer. The mother who works full-time in this first critical year is placing her baby at risk no matter how dedicated Grandma may be! And in the current discussion on children's rights the right to maternal care and affection should head the list. The need for this closeness has been emphasized by Paul Adams, and it has been demonstrated by Rene Spitz in the United States, by D. W. Winnicott and James Robertson in England—as well as by countless mothers in every generation the world over.[2]

There are two broad points of view about the care and rearing of babies. The methods are known by the names of their High Priests—Dr Spock and Truby King, the latter perhaps more familiar to present-day grand-parents, though his ideas live on.

Dr Spock, the American pediatrician, has had a greater impact on child rearing than any other individual in the past quarter century. His *Pocket Book* has sold over 20 million copies throughout the world.[3] Every page is crammed with good sense and good advice. It is the one book which should be essential reading for all parents and teachers of young children. His advice to parents: "You know more than you think. . . . Don't be afraid to trust your instincts—the natural loving care that kindly parents give their children is a hundred times more valuable than knowing how to pin a nappy on just right or how to make up a feed expertly." This is at the centre of his philosophy. Given a mother's instinctive good sense in meeting her child's needs for food, comfort and love, it doesn't really matter much whether she is moderately strict or moderately permissive. The issue to Dr Spock is not strictness or permissiveness, but whether a child's needs are being met, emotional as well as physical, and whether, as a result, he is growing up with happiness and confidence.

Dr Spock's *Baby and Child Care* has recently appeared in a Russian translation and has attracted some criticism from Academician Nikolai Amosov because, he says, it does not stress sufficiently the positive influence on a young child that his parents' initiative can have.

Sir Truby King (1858–1938) was a warm-hearted New Zealander who studied medicine at Edinburgh, served in the Royal Infirmaries of Glasgow and Edinburgh, and then returned to New Zealand, where he became for the next thirty years medical superintendent of a mental hospital near Dunedin. He humanized the hospital regime, abandoned authoritarian practices and developed the therapy of craftwork, gardening, and farmwork. Indeed it was from his interest in the scientific rearing of plants and animals, particularly calves, that he acquired a passionate and life-long interest in the rearing of babies. By scientific feeding he considerably reduced the mortality rate from diarrhoea among the calves on the asylum's farm. He then pointed out that the lives of 1,000 children a year could be saved in New Zealand if similar attention were paid by the Government to instructing mothers how to feed their children correctly. Within five years of the formation of The Truby King Society in New Zealand the deaths from epidemic summer diarrhoea fell from 25 to 9 per 1,000, and in the following five years to 1 per 1,000. The purpose of the Society was not only to reduce the infant mortality rate but to ensure the maximum development, health and well-being of those who survived. Its methods were based upon breast feeding to the ninth month, strictly controlled diet afterwards, regularity in everything, fresh air and sunlight galore and a very high standard of hygiene.

The Truby King system, evolved over thirty years, became the vogue in many countries—indeed the Preface to the Eighth Edition of *Mothercraft*, the bible of the cult, states that it was published ". . . to meet the needs of mothers throughout the British Empire."![4]

Unfortunately both Spock and Truby King suffered from the zeal and worse, the heresy, of their disciples—the fate of all prophets. Their teachings have acquired a gloss which bears little relation to the work on which they were based. Truby King became identified with the authoritarian don't-pick-him-up school. Leila Berg has described what was made of his methods by middle-class parents in Britain after the first world war.[2] The regularity on which he insisted was elevated into a stern creed often excluding the warm-hearted link between mother and child which is the first and deepest need of every baby. Crying was good for him. He must be fed every four hours, not a minute more or less, even at 2 a.m.! He must be left outside in his pram in all weathers—even when the snow was piled high on the hood. No cuddling—too namby-pamby, anyhow—think of the danger of infection! Hygiene and the clock imposed a rigid, often loveless regime on many homes.

Michael was a Truby King baby but not subjected to the rigours which too often debased the methods which, in New Zealand, had improved child care out of all recognition.

On the other hand Spock's emphasis on trusting the mother's natural love and instinct also degenerated among American mothers, but in the opposite direction—towards extreme permissiveness. "Meeting the child's needs" came to mean pandering to his every whim.

The sensible approach is to look behind both extremes at the real Truby King and the real Spock. Spock's emphasis on love and meeting the child's needs as the most effective guides to mothering is supported by the work of a long succession of educationists such as Dewey, psychologists such as Freud, and pediatricians such as Gesell and Aldrich. The work in the United States on self-demand schedules of Dr Preston McLendon and Mrs Frances P. Simsarian also supports his theories.[3] Like Truby King, Spock also found a considerable balance of argument in favour of breast-feeding, though living in a time, unlike the 1920s, when bottle-feeding can be safe and free from infection, he is less obsessive about it.

Truby King's insistence on correct diet and healthy surroundings has had massive support in recent years in many investigations into the relationship between environmental deprivation and child development which are discussed in Chapter 4.

The norms of child development, i.e. the relationship between age and the stage of growth reached, are of great value in the study of childhood for two reasons. First, the needs of children which the mother, and later the teacher, are there to meet are determined by them. An obvious example is the kind of toys and play material needed at any given age. These must be appropriate to the stage of development if they are to assist and not hinder it. Secondly, they enable both mother and teacher to compare the individual child with the average for his age. This can be of considerable importance, e.g. in assessing the effects of congenital defects, of social deprivation, or of long illness—provided we remember that he is only being compared with the average and that it is normal to diverge from it in both directions.

Most mothers pay considerable attention to the norm for weight. A visit to the clinic will show just how much importance they attach to every ounce gained or lost. They do not bother nearly so much about the no less important norms for mental development. But again it must be stressed that these norms like those for weight have been arrived at by studying large numbers of individual children. It is important to remember, especially for the anxious mother whose child may not be keeping up developmentally with the Joneses, that the "average" child does not exist. There are wide differences in growth and development.

The brief outline of growth and development which follows is based upon observations of American children by Arnold Gesell.[5]

At birth no creature is quite so helpless or incomplete as the baby. It has been said that he is not fully born until the age of four weeks. He is totally demanding both physically and emotionally, and completely inconsiderate. His presence demands an immediate adaptation to his needs by both parents, an identification with him and an almost superhuman effort to see things from his point of view. This comes naturally enough to the mother but is much more difficult for the father.

At birth he certainly appears to exhibit desires and even love, hate and anger. He can move his head. Twelve days after Michael was born he could hold his head up in the bath. There is evidence that his intellectual growth begins almost immediately after birth. His fingers can grip but his eyes move independently of each other. From the very moment of birth his mouth is quite obviously more than merely the channel for food but, as Susan Isaacs has pointed out, the very centre of his mental life.[6] The only elements in his environment which possess reality for him are those which his lips tell him are real. It is a remaining physical link with his mother. Sucking is his source of love as well as food. His rudimentary mental life is adapted to her and not to the outside world.

Within one or two days, almost simultaneously, his mouth will unmistakably seek the breast at the same time as his eyes will seek the light. These are his first self-sought contacts with the world outside the womb—mankind's twin sources of life. It is almost as though what he "learns" with his mouth he applies to his eyes.

About the same time there emerges a vague awareness of space and his hands begin to grasp for the moon, a characteristic he will never outgrow! His spontaneous movements visibly increase from one day to another—in the first week apparently utterly chaotic but, after that, with some dim but apparent purpose behind them.

At the end of a month he can bring his head from the side to a mid position when lying on his back. He will often extend his legs, arms and fingers in what appears to the new mother to be a rather terrifying paroxysm of stretching. He stares at "nothing" for long periods. He can focus his eyes now and will follow a bunch of keys overhead—but with head as well as eyes. It is not recorded that Michael did this until his fifty-seventh day. So much for the norm! His hands are much less skilful than his eyes and he has not learnt to grasp the keys or even attempt to do so. Nevertheless there are more and more experimental movements of the body as the muscles develop. There is also some response to sounds—not a perceptual response but an obvious awareness of them. He is beginning to be aware of things going on around him.

As the weeks pass co-ordination of hand and eye begins to emerge and at four weeks the dangled bunch of keys will set in motion crude, indeed chaotic, but very enthusiastic movements of eyes, hands, legs and hands. Great excitement! His earliest notions of space, the near space in his pram or cot, are appearing. At this age Michael played frequently with woolly balls hanging at the side of his pram. He did not start taking an interest in the braid along the edges until the twelfth week. He will enjoy sitting up with a back-rest and looking around him. Michael did not sit up in his pram until the thirtieth week. Gesell believes that this is more than pleasure at a new posture but it is a widening of his horizons generally and, therefore, a new social orientation. Sitting up makes the world a bigger place with a different perspective, though he will not understand the mysteries of its wider spaces until he walks in his second year.

He will now hold and examine objects placed in his hands. He will play with his fingers and try to pull them off. His perceptual ability, seen in his recognition of familiar objects, is growing daily. At five weeks Michael was taking a great interest in the tall trees outside the house. On a train journey in his thirteenth week he insisted on looking out of the window all the way. The repertoire of noises has developed enormously and now includes a wide range of sounds. Michael's first recorded sounds were "ah-oo"—"ah-gey" in his second month. He did not say "ba-ba" until the thirty-fifth week, and "da-da" two weeks later. At thirteen months his favourite noise was "Yath" and at fourteen months it was "good-good." The repertoire of sounds will include laughter evoked by a familiar figure and so the first beginnings of socializing outside his relationship with his mother emerge. He is beginning to acquire relationships with others—his father and his brothers and sisters. Michael's first recorded smile was forty-two days after birth. He laughed aloud first in his twelfth week, and again in his fourteenth week. After that frequently.

During the longer waking periods of his second six months he becomes predominantly a sitter—indeed he is by now half way to standing. He can grasp an object on sight with one hand and put it into the other. His visual apprehension is still well-ahead of his manual skill, but co-ordination between the two continues to improve rapidly. He is now an avid inspector and manipulator of objects. Because of his intense interest in objects at this age he can amuse himself in a sustained way for quite long periods. It is the most self-contained period of early infancy. To his immediate post-natal instrument of exploration, his mouth, he has now added eyes and hands. And to taste, sight and feeling in getting to know things he now increasingly adds the sound, as when he bangs things on the floor. But the senses of taste, touch and smell remain even at this age his most vivid way of knowing about objects. And he needs a great variety of things to feel, handle and drop.

His growing knowledge of his toys and their qualities is matched by an increasing acquaintance with his friends and with the daily routine of his home. An extract from Michael's diary at eighteen weeks: "Michael fed the two rabbits today. He gave them each a lettuce leaf. His eyes nearly popped out in wonder!" He, the rabbits and a tortoise, quickly became firm friends. At this age the baby's interest in and understanding of his world are increasing by leaps and bounds for the development of his mind is closely connected with the growth and development of his body.

At the same time his vocal experiments become more diverse and more adventurous. No words will have come out of the jumble of sounds, but the phonetic ingredients of speech will all be there mixed up in an enchanting jumble. (See Chapter 3.)

It is in the third quarter that he may experience the second major disturbance of his life. Birth was the first; weaning is the second. And this is much more than a change of diet. It severs the last precious physical link with his genesis and because of this, unless it is delayed until he can feel his mother's love in other ways, it may cause retardation of development accompanied by symptoms such as thumb-sucking.

At the beginning of the last quarter of his first year he can get from the lying to the sitting position and he may be able to crawl. Michael was making strenuous efforts to crawl as early as the twentieth week. At thirty weeks he was trying still harder but could only move in a circle. By the ninth month he could move quickly across the floor by a dragging movement, and by the tenth month he could pull himself up to a standing position in his play-pen. At this age the baby can pull himself up into a standing position, for his legs, feet, toes, as well as fingers, are now rapidly coming under his control and, with experiment, becoming stronger. But he will not yet have the balance to stand without holding, though his legs will carry his whole weight.

He will show a remarkable interest in very tiny things such as crumbs, and he will be able to pick them up with thumb and forefinger. For the first time he displays an awareness of more than one object or person at a time. This vague comprehension of the wooden spoon *and* the empty can, of mother *and* father, of the empty tin *and* the noise it makes when banged—of two-ness—marks his most considerable intellectual advance to date from the helpless creature he was at birth to the intelligent little person he will shortly become. His leap forward will later grow into perceptual and intellectual ability.

The development of the outlying parts of the nervous system affecting the extremities of tongue, fingers and toes has an important bearing on the emergence of speech. He is now conscious of his tongue, indeed it has become an object of play, he gets hold of it and tries to pull it out, and this, together with his love of trying new sounds brings him almost to the threshold of speech. He becomes a mimic. At this age Michael's pram stood daily in a garden over which an electricity cable ran. It was a favourite roost of starlings and he imitated their shrill calls with remarkable accuracy. He may also be able to say, without comprehension of course, "Ma-ma" or "Da-da." He will almost certainly "know" his name.

On his first birthday he creeps skilfully and will have developed his own distinctive style of doing so. He can walk with support but probably cannot stand alone until thirteen months. He can throw a ball—a considerable achievement involving the co-ordination of its release by his fingers with the swing of the arm. Similarly he can place an object into a box. He is beginning to appreciate relationships between things more accurately and can place a series of objects on the table. This is another leap forward for it is the first step to counting.

He is now a really adventurous explorer, particularly when he begins to walk a little. What he does is now clearly intentional and experimental. Trial and error are his established method of finding out and each new achievement gives him obvious pleasure, e.g. when he learns a new word or climbs on to an armchair. He will repeat the word or trick endlessly.

If he is an only child or a late child in a grown-up family his socializimg may have reached the point where he dominates the family. He now knows his own family; he laughs with them and at them, he responds to a number of words and phrases and (parents beware!) he has become extremely sensitive to tones of voice. Babies and dogs can sense meaning from tone of voice to a quite remarkable degree. And he is an entertainer. He amuses his family with his antics and greatly enjoys doing so, and appears to know that they also enjoy it. In fact while he is becoming a person in his own right with an identity of his own paradoxically he needs companionship more and more, particularly in his play. Companionship is the key to, and context of, personal identity.

By the middle of his second year he has made considerable physical progress both in growth and in bodily control, and he will not be walking now with the stiff gait of a few months earlier. He can even crawl upstairs and come down bottom first. Michael did not walk alone until the fifteenth month, but he displayed considerable skill at it almost immediately. Aspects of intellectual and emotional growth are less obvious than, say, his twelve teeth. It may be for this reason, as Gesell has pointed out, that this transitional period from babyhood to infancy is the least understood by parents. There is an apparent imbalance between rapid physical growth and less obvious psychological development.

He can now place two, sometimes three, bricks on top of each other without trial and error. He is clearly acquiring a sense of the vertical but not, as yet, of the horizontal. He can turn over the pages of a book, and obviously recognizes pictures of familiar objects. He loves to scribble freely, and can imitate vertical strokes. He can point to parts of his body and familiar objects when asked to do so. At thirteen months Michael could point out his favourite picture of a baby when asked "Where's the baby?"

His approach towards counting develops from a preoccupation with ones, simple objects, through the awareness of twoness, to the assembling of piles of small things. He will scatter them at a stroke, and then carefully reassemble them.

Linguistically he will have progressed to about ten normally clear words and a rich flow of jargon. He will also understand simple, often-repeated commands.

He is extremely egocentric and conservative and dislikes sudden changes of routine. For this reason he will often, because of his immaturity, appear to be a dreadful little rebel, but this requires understanding. It is one of the norms of his development. Stern, authoritarian discipline is the worst possible attitude towards the rebelliousness of the two-year-old.

Perceptually he has made a great deal of progress. Since his first birthday he is beginning to dissociate things from his actions; the world is acquiring a permanence and a detachment from him; it is no longer an extension of him. He is acquiring his own inner model of the world built at this age only from his own limited experience. All he knows of any other objects around him or the familiar events in his routine has been acquired from his own activities, particularly his play, in relation to them. In fact his play is his thinking and it is of such overwhelming importance in child development that Chapter 2 is devoted entirely to it.

The major changes between the middle and end of his second year, apart from the physical growth of four more teeth and three more pounds, are the growth of language and the development of personality. He still looks top-heavy, like the primitive little man he is, but his muscular development and control have made enormous progress. His play is rough and active. He delights in the running, jumping, dancing, shouting or any kind of crude acrobatics.

His hands and fingers are much more skilful; e.g. he can use scissors and string beads. He can now place six bricks on top of each other—a great advance in six months. More important still, his experimentation with bricks enters another dimension at two years. As well as vertical building he can now place them horizontally in a row to make a train. He will not be able to combine the vertical and the horizontal by putting a chimney on the train for another six months. Similarly in his scribbling he can imitate a horizontal stroke for the first time. He will not yet be able to distinguish colours—apart from black and white.

Vocabulary growth will have been quite remarkable. He may know some hundreds of words, mainly nouns, and will only resort to his earlier jargon when words fail him, as they often will. He will love repetition accompanied by sing-song almost to the point of driving his family frantic! Simple stories about himself will fascinate him, but more sophisticated stories will mean nothing to him. From these and his repetitive sing-song chants he will learn to use other parts of speech.

The personal pronouns *mine* and *me* will now be in constant use and indicate a firmly established feeling of personal identity, that he is a person, as well as a sense of possession. For this reason he will appear to be a selfish little creature. But as his own sense of identity grows the identity of others becomes clearer. This is particularly the case with his mother, with whom his special symbiotic links finally fall away in the second year. The joys of dependence give way to those of autonomy.

At the age of two his socialization has reached the point where he is capable of acquiring a sense of guilt, at any rate superficially. And there is a great temptation to the mother to use this capacity for feeling guilt for her own convenience. Indeed what Paul Adams calls "the repertoire of child subjugation" really "takes" in the second year.[2] Examples are witholding of rewards, restriction of movement, shaming, bullying, telling-off, etc. All put the two-year-old's personality development at risk.

The watershed of three is normally the start of nursery school or playgroup. Two is too young. It is probably the most attractive age in childhood. The three-year-old is wise and serious, yet at the same time appallingly ignorant of the big world outside his home, maybe in a multi-storey block of flats, a secluded middle-class home in the suburbs or a slum tenement. The new wonders which surround him on every side in the playgroup or nursery school cause great confusions for him and he commits the most colossal bloomers, yet he has a tremendous capacity to learn and assimilate experience rapidly from them.

Massive muscular activity still gives him pleasure, and he can stand on one foot for a little while. His movements generally are more controlled. This is seen in his skill in running, turning at speed and stopping suddenly at play out of doors. He is now of age to pedal a tricycle. He can feed himself unaided and usually both dress and undress himself, including the fastening of buttons. But he now also enjoys longer spells sitting on the floor in quiet absorption with his play rather like his self-contained period in his second six months. He is indeed capable of sustained activity in pursuit of one desired objective. He gets a more sophisticated pleasure from his crayons. Previously it was mainly the motor activity of scribbling which he liked, but now he begins to draw spontaneously with an increasing degree of definition. His brick-building, both vertical and horizontal, has further improved over a year ago. Although both dimensions are now familiar he shows no capacity for the oblique plane in drawing, paper-folding or building; e.g. he cannot copy a cross made from two oblique lines.

He has more accurate perception of space and form and can match the three basic shapes, square, circle and triangle, without difficulty, though probably not colours. He can go a step further and classify simple objects from their shapes—and this is another major intellectual stride forward.

Indeed his perceptual development now leaps ahead with the aid of a growing use and understanding of words and an incessant stream of questions. His vocabulary may even contain one thousand words. He very readily responds to words and commands including the prepositions which indicate a relationship between one thing and another. He talks to himself and almost always dramatizes in his play. He still gets great pleasure from chanting and repetition. All this verbal activity improves and defines his capacity for language, but it also enables him to think in words rather than in motor sensory terms as he did earlier. It is this rapidly growing capacity to use and be influenced by the words of others that gives the three-year-old the aura of maturity and his disarming charm.

But, of course, it is a capacity which can only develop in an environment which encourages the growth of language, where neither mother nor teacher ever tires of the often apparently meaningless and seemingly endless questioning which fills most of his waking hours, where he is talked to and told stories of a type which are appropriate to three years of age. (See Chapter 3.) Deprivation of this or any other kind really begins to show at three.

Coincidental with his responsiveness to words is a remarkable desire to please, to help, to co-operate, to conform. His emotions are strong, and may surface in intense but brief outbursts of anger, fear, anxiety or jealousy, which may be expressed in words but, more often in more primitive, physical ways. In spite of his growing socialization he still plays mainly in parallel with other children rather than with them.

A year later his bodily dexterity has improved and he may even be able to skip though not to hop. He takes a new and keen interest in physical feats, both massive, athletic ones and those involving more precise movements.

At long last he is beginning to experiment in the oblique dimension but he probably cannot yet copy a cross of two obliques, but he can copy one with vertical and horizontal lines: + but not ×.

His questioning is no less compulsive than a year ago, but its purpose is now not so much to *find* out as to *sort* out. His concepts are gaining in depth and accuracy as he organizes his experience. The factual content of questions and answers is less important than how they can be fitted into the pattern of what he already knows.

He has no very accurate sense of past and present yet, but he is a young man of considerable achievements. His memory has developed but not beyond counting to four. Simple stories about children like himself still enthral him, but those with plots do not interest him. He will probably follow the narrative with physical gestures—he still to some extent thinks with his body. He can draw a man but usually with head and limbs but no body. He can match up to ten forms and create buildings with bricks which involve both dimensions.

His own answers to questions are often inordinately long. A simple question may release a flood of associated thinking, and it is important that no attempt should be made to close the gate, for what in an adult would be garrulity in a four-year-old is an essential stage in sorting out and conceptualizing his own experience. On it his future intellectual development depends. He can tell long involved stories and make excuses which are part fact and part fiction. In Gesell's view the very fact that he makes excuses indicates his growing socialization. What others think of him is becoming important—hence the need to make excuses.

He is now a social being but still with a wide streak of independence—indeed he is often independent and assertive to a rather trying degree.

In his play with a group there is a good deal more real contact with others at four, but he may, on occasions, deliberately provoke them in order to experience their reaction. He can be extremely dictatorial in his attitudes towards other children.

Like the three-year-old he is still subject to intense and increasing fears, often for no obvious reason and of the most unlikely things, a reminder that he is not quite as grown-up as he may sound. All in all he is a lively creative little boy—given the right kind of environment. His endless questioning, his assertiveness, his inability to distinguish fact from fiction must be endured with understanding as another essential stage in the growth towards maturity.

Five marks the end of early childhood. In this country it is the beginning of statutory school life and, for this reason, a myth has been created that at this age the child should be ready for all the mysteries of literacy and numeracy. He may be or he may not be ready to read for another two years—or he may already be reading. How much parental worry could be avoided if this was more widely understood—if only parents could learn to wait for the right moment!

But he is well established in his little world. He understands a great deal about it and his own identity in it as well as the identity of others. He is now more concerned with reality than with magic. Physically his control and balance are more sophisticated, accurate and confident. His sense of rhythm has also appeared, indeed this is the age to begin to learn to dance. He can use tools and crayons more skilfully and can now draw oblique lines without difficulty. His drawings of men now have bodies as well as heads and limbs and are much more complete in detail. Indeed in many respects he has, for the first time, a general feeling for completing things—drawings, games, stories, etc. He likes to see it all wound up tidily at the end. He can probably count to ten. His memory and sense of time are developing.

Clearly an idea formulated in his mind now more often than not precedes action. This is seen vividly in drawing, where he knows what he is going to draw before he draws it, compared with a year ago when he decided what it was after it was finished or during its execution—a technique which is not unknown in modern art.

He asks fewer questions but what he does ask are more to the point than in the previous two years. They are asked primarily for information and not to enable him to sort out his experiences. He now uses complete sentences and, structurally, his language is complete. He knows about two thousand words unless his home is linguistically impoverished. His play dramatizes mainly the intensely practical business of everyday adult life and it does so with an excessive amount of commentary—shopping, making meals, the doctor's visit, etc. He uses his verbal skill to the full to improve his understanding of the world. This putting of familiar situations into words is much more in the form of monologues than of genuine conversation and the interchange of ideas—although he now plays reasonably happily in small groups. He loves to help around the house or the school and can do so competently.

But in spite of his great strides forward in physical control, perception, conceptualization, language and independence, he is still egocentric, still unable to reason, still extremely immature—particularly emotionally.

But in spite of this immaturity the little boy who leaves the nursery school and presents himself at the infant school is pleasant, co-operative, conformist, intensely practical and self-assured and easy to get along with.

2. Play

The most engaging quality of young children is their capacity for play—a capacity which they share with the young of most mammals. "The elusive sprite," Sir Percy Nunn called it.[7] The nursery school child plays with his toys, the kitten with a piece of wool, the puppy with a ball and the young lambs obviously enjoy their chaotic races.

The length of the period in the life of a young mammal when play is the dominant activity appears to be in direct proportion both to the time taken to reach maturity and to the ability to learn patterns of behaviour which are not inherited. The play of the lamb is short-lived. It quickly reaches maturity, learns nothing new and soon behaves as sheep have always behaved. The pattern of sheep behaviour is genetically determined and virtually incapable of change. The puppy is capable of learning a great deal more and retains the capacity for play until the old dog can learn no more tricks. The kitten lies somewhere between the two.

The young human being on the other hand normally retains his enjoyment of play unimpaired for the first two decades of life and, in most cases, keeps it to some extent throughout life. Man's capacity for, and obvious need of, play far exceeds that of any other creature—and he is Lord of Creation surpassing all the animals in his knowledge, skill and adaptability. And there is a close connection between his play and his achievements. The child's future, what he makes of himself, the kind of person he becomes is, of course, partly the result of his genetic inheritance but, to a considerable extent, it is also due to such factors as environment, education and training and is capable of a good deal of modification.

There does appear to be a clear connection between the play phenomenon in the young and the degree of modification which is possible in their inherited adult patterns of behaviour. The lamb cannot change its inheritance; the child can. "Play makes adaptation possible."[8] If this is true between one species of animal and another it is a reasonable assumption that it applies also between one child and another. The more a child plays the more he learns.

The sheer absorption of young children in their own affairs—the baby with his rattle, the girl with her dolls, the boy with tools and boxes—is an indication of the depth of their being which is involved in play. Observation of the play of children tells more about them than almost anything else. It provides the clearest and most unmistakable evidence that play is an essential part in the process of growing up—of acquiring skill, knowledge, understanding, identity in society; that it is nature's own device for enabling the world and its mysteries to become known and "assimilated" (Piaget's term). It is the great educator. And because of this, understanding of it must be central to the professional knowledge of every teacher and playgroup leader, indeed, their training and study should have the play phenomenon as its centre of gravity. Nature has shown us how the child learns and adapts, and we should be foolish indeed to ignore its method. Rousseau understood the importance of play in the development of children. Froebel based his system of education from experience upon it, and the modern primary school uses it as the dynamic of all its methods.

It is an aspect of human growth and of education which has for long intrigued teachers and psychologists. At least four theories have been evolved to explain it. There are two psychological theories, the first of which has come to be known as the "surplus energy" theory, of Schiller (1875) and Spencer (1872). Unfortunately it is also the theory of many mothers and some teachers today. It takes the view that there is generated in the young and in some adults a surplus of energy which is expended in spontaneous activities which are quite independent of external stimuli. We may add to this view the fact that the surplus energy is being used in order to prepare for adult life. However, even with the addition, the theory is inadequate to explain the discovery of new sources of energy by the tired child when a dreary task is changed into a game—a change which is familiar to every teacher.

There is, therefore, another almost opposite popular interpretation of play as a mechanism used when energy is at a low ebb in order to restore and recreate it—hence the term "recreation."

There are also two biological interpretations. The philosopher Malebranche first suggested the rather obvious "preparation for life" theory which was elaborated by Karl Groos (1895), whose ideas, together with those of Piaget, have been extremely influential in the harnessing of play in educational methods. He saw the kitten chasing its tail as a preparation for hunting the mouse or the bird; the three-year-old girl with her doll as a mother in the making. To him play was anticipatory of the serious business of life, and, therefore, involved the unending make-believe of childhood. His views have been developed in more recent years by Professor Huizinga (1949) and Roger Caillois (1961). Both saw play as having a significance far beyond itself. Caillois believed it essential for the development and socialization of children.

The second biological interpretation is the "recapitulation" theory of Professor Stanley Hall (1905). He interpreted the play of childhood as a recapitulation of the history of the race—imaginary hunting, building dens, etc. He believed that the playing out by each generation in childhood of racial memories was necessary to healthy adult life. The primaeval forest was still in the make-up of each child, with all its brutishness, but by play it was cleansed and sublimated into socially acceptable channels.

There was really no conflict between Groos and Hall, although Hall was very critical of his predecessor. They emphasized different aspects of play. There does appear to be evidence that the play of childhood springs from the racial memory, indeed children in widely separated and different countries and cultures develop similar play forms without any prompting from parents or teachers, and they did so before the mass media started to iron out cultural differences by encouraging imitation. But it is equally likely that the memory stirs anew in each generation of children because the enacting of it is not only cathartic—cleansing the ancient vices—but also a preparation for adult life.

But the greatest contribution to thinking on the purpose of childhood play has been made by Piaget. He did not believe it was anticipatory but that the main purpose was to enable the child to live in a secure world of his own—secure because he controls it by his magic and make-believe. From this secure base he gradually comes to terms with the real world of things, people and ideas, by assimilating his experience of them. It is a private reality of his own in which he lives securely until he can accommodate to the sterner reality of the world of adults.

Piaget distinguished three types of play in this process of assimilation and accommodation, which will be familiar to the mother who has watched the play of her child change as he grows older. First games involving the practice of physical skills, then symbolic play involving make-believe and finally play involving others—social play with group-enforced rules. From the sheer joy of repeating acquired physical skills e.g. knocking the woollen balls on the pram, through his own world of magic he finally acquires sufficient experience to come to terms with the social world. The connection between the play phenomenon and the process of socialization is of major importance in the education of young children.

The connection was developed by Helanko who saw socialization as the product not of uninterrupted play but of the alternation of play and non-play. He also stressed, as Piaget had done, the therapeutic value of play—the retreat from the stress of reality in the adult world to a reality of childhood.

Among all these views on the function of play there is agreement that it is essential to the growth, development and socialization of children, that it is spontaneous, independent of external needs and should, therefore, be regarded as an aspect of a particular piece of behaviour, not as an isolated phenomenon, but one which gives meaning to the behaviour of children.

Its importance in education is now widely accepted but frequently misunderstood, because the play phenomenon in young children is as fragile as a dream, and if it is over-consciously pursued and exploited, "play or else," it will vanish like a dream. The so-called "play-way" methods, to use an old term, are like trying to "catch a moonbeam in your hand."

The important thing is to provide a secure context in which young children can safely retreat into their own world of magic and also to make available to them the resources on which the magic and make-believe can function. The adult is usually free of his circumstances only in his thinking, but the young child should be able to roam through his own special world uninhibited by adult reality. He is a magician who can create or change whatever he will—the cardboard box into a ship or an aeroplane; the broomstick into a pony; the blocks into houses. And to him the ship, the aeroplane, the pony and the houses are real. To doubt their reality is to strip him of his security. "Play is a serious business."[3] A whiff of adult anger, impatience, disbelief, or even indifference is all that is needed to destroy the world of fancy. In play the child must choose for himself. He knows what is best for himself, although he may often need and ask for the help of adults. Imposed play is always counter-productive.

The world of play is one which every mother and teacher should know and feel about, respect and protect with understanding and sympathy. The magician of three may grow into the scientist of thirty. But he is unlikely to do so if his childhood world of make-believe is regarded as "fibbing" or "day-dreaming." One of the most important contributions the mother or nursery teacher can make to the richness and security of the child's world is by providing the kind of play material which lends itself to imagination and make-believe, and which provides a stimulus to play. The perfect-in-every-detail coloured plastic replica does not give scope for the exercise of the imagination in the same way as boxes, blocks, sand, water, scraps of material, etc., do. The more realistic they are, the less they leave to the imagination.

Most pre-school children prefer kitchen utensils to expensively contrived "educational" toys. This is probably partly because they are usually of simple design and robust material; for example, a spoon or an aluminium pan, but also because they are mother's "toys," and even the one-year old will want to imitate mother. The parents or local education authorities who buy expensive, complicated toys for their young children do them a disservice. What is important is a great variety of simple, safe material, always including wooden bricks of different colours and sizes—the most versatile material of all for magic. The need for simplicity applies equally to dolls—for the very young child a soft woolly type and for the nursery years a washable one—hair included! Similarly with trains. How many fond fathers have bored their children to death with clockwork trains complete with lines? Given a good supply of bricks the child will use his magic to make his own train—an adaptable train which he can manipulate with ease. And it is worth remembering that he always pushes before he pulls. Given this kind of train in the early years he may reach the stage in later childhood when a clockwork or an electric train will have an appeal, but to try to force the pace on trains, dolls, or anything else is to impair his confidence in himself and to detract from his competence as a great magician.

Michael had a relative who persisted in buying him Dinky cars from the age of two. At that age they meant nothing to him as cars, but he was fascinated by the tyres which he learnt to remove with great skill by the age of 30 months, and which he then used for other purposes. There is an important lesson in this. If a young child has an over-sophisticated toy the sensible parent will allow him to use it in his own way, and it will rarely be the way intended by the manufacturer!

Young children need things to push and pull, turn over and upside down, take to pieces, throw about. The texture, size, weight, colour, even the smell, should vary. Their thirst for knowledge through experience is insatiable. And it is important to realize what is important to them; for example, the first feel of a new surface texture such as velvet or polystyrene is as important and exciting a new experience to a young child as a first flight in an aeroplane to a teenager.

Pre-school education, whether in the home or the nursery school, is to a considerable extent a matter of providing the resources with which the child can educate himself through play and make-believe. The variety of play material which can be provided quite inexpensively, for most of it is household material, is almost limitless. But there are a number of old favourites according to the age of the child, which have their appeal in every generation and every country—the irreducible minimum —with which he will create a world of magic in which his skills, his language, and his thinking will develop. In it he will also come to the brink of reading and counting.

The baby needs a succession of simple objects, starting with a plastic ring or rattle or two rings tied together with tape, which can be explored with hands, eyes, mouth, nose and ears—not objects with specific functions, but those which are versatile enough to allow this multi-dimensional, multi-sensory, exploration. Think of all the uses to which a baby can put a plastic ring or a spoon!

As soon as he begins to crawl his toys must be of the kind which can be as mobile as he is, e.g. those which roll or can be pushed or pulled. Very soon the sophistication of wheeled objects begins to make its appeal. Considering the relationship between some men and their cars it appears to be one which is lifelong! A simple wooden truck is attractive at this age and for some time to come, and if it has a robust handle it has the added attraction of helping to steady the toddler as he begins to stand and walk. Michael had a life-sized fox terrier on wheels but he always insisted on using it end up and sitting on its upturned, horizontal neck.

The truck, like all the toys of early childhood, serves other purposes; e.g. towards the end of the first year when the two-ness of things attracts his interest he will put something into it and, for him, the two will go together. A little later he will fill it with other small objects.

Simple wooden or plastic bricks are perhaps the most universally useful play materials of all. They should be of varying sizes and colours—though he probably will not be able to distinguish the colours until the end of his second year. Towards the end of the first year bricks are particularly important, with other small objects, to assemble in piles and then scatter across the room. They are placed on the table one at a time in the second year, an important exercise in developing spatial relationships, but, perhaps most important of all, they are used to build in the horizontal and vertical planes and, later, to combine the two in the ship with a funnel. And so—bricks of all shapes, sizes and colours from six months to five years.

The world's most successful toy, Lego (Danish *leg godt,* "play well") is an interlocking plastic brick invented by Ole Christiansen and his son Godtfrid. It was first shown at the Nuremberg toy fair in 1954. The toy dealers laughed. "Bricks are finished," they said indulgently. "You should try rocket-ships, ray-guns, dolls." In 1958 £1 million worth of Lego were sold, in 1961 £6 million, and in 1972 £30 million.[9]

A soft, light ball should be among the first birthday presents. Throwing it is a big step forward in co-ordination. At the same time, or shortly afterwards, a strong brightly-coloured picture book with simple bold pictures will be increasingly treasured. Pictures of children cut out of magazines will stimulate a great deal of very important pre-language baby-talk.

Throughout the whole pre-school period from the first half of the second year onwards, there should be constant opportunity for play and experiment with water, sand (wet and dry), dough and, later, clay. The endless experimentation with objects and malleable material of this kind is an essential part of early education. Unfortunately in many modern homes, through lack of space or because of an obsessively houseproud mother, this vital activity is not possible or not permitted.

Towards the end of the second year more sophisticated operations, such as stringing beads or cutting paper with non-dangerous scissors, are possible. At this age also play becomes rougher, involving dancing, running and climbing, and demands space as well as things to conquer, such as armchairs and settees. And confidence grows with each conquest.

Simple drawing materials (waxed crayons and pencils are the most suitable) are as much part of the staple play material as bricks—but large sheets of paper are essential. Newspaper is admirable. But any attempt to help the young child to draw or paint an object more accurately will kill his joy and spontaneity stone-dead. The more accurate house or man in his drawings will appear in due season. To attempt to "teach" him to draw will impair a most valuable part of his early education. And it is worth repeating that this is a rule with wide application in the education of young children. Nature has a time for everything. Don't try to improve on it.

Similarly, the fond parents who provide a tricycle before the age of three are wasting their money. The co-ordination required for pedalling develops quite naturally at three.

Also at about three dressing-up as mother, father, the doctor or the nurse becomes a major form of play, and lots of material should always be available for this playing out of adult roles. In every generation little girls have loved to wear their mothers' shoes and little boys their fathers' hats! And this is just as important in the home as in the nursery school. Related to this is the desire to help mother or teacher—baking utensils, the miniature carpet-sweeper, polishing materials, etc., have a never-failing appeal to the three-to-five-year-olds.

Traditionally the nursery class has set aside an area as a "home corner" with its table, chairs, crockery, armchair, and all the props for playing at homes. As with toys, it is far better to delineate the "house" with large, light polystyrene blocks which are easily moved and adaptable to the drama of the moment, and it is frequently changing, than to use the over-detailed Wendy House of a few years ago with its painted bricks, red roofing tiles, curtained windows and roses over the door. The first rule about play material is that the simpler it is the more useful it is to the child because his imagination is not inhibited by fussy details.

With increasing bodily mastery and mobility the nursery school child needs facilities for physical feats in which he delights and which do a great deal both to build his confidence and to develop muscular co-ordination; e.g. at the nursery school at Knottingley in the West Riding of Yorkshire there are good examples of outdoor play sculpture for this purpose. These include a grassed amphitheatre, large cement pipes through the wall for crawling, wood-covered walls to sit or walk on, up-ended cement slabs, etc.

The educational supply industry has produced a great variety of ingenious and safe climbing apparatus suitable for the 3–5 age-group.

Beyond this irreducible minimum successful nursery classes and playgroups provide a great variety of toys, equipment and play material—some of it commercially manufactured but a great deal from waste material accumulated by teachers and parents. And in the throw-away society in which we are living a rich and varied collection can be made without difficulty.

The following is a list of all material available in the very successful nursery class attached to the Ravenswood Infant School, Newcastle-upon-Tyne. It includes furniture and domestic equipment, indeed the complete contents of the two interconnected rooms used by the class, as it is impossible to draw a clear line between what is specifically provided as play material and what is not. The child's capacity for play uses everything available, the tables and chairs no less than the bricks and sand.

Toys and bought material

jigsaws
lotto
picture lotto
colour factor
stickle bricks
wooden beads and laces
sorting trays
nesting boxes
nesting toys
graduated trays
grading toys
giant Lego (Duplo)
Pennybrix; Matador; Picabrix
Fitbits; Bildit
garage, cars and car tracks
farm animals (plastic)
soldiers and fort
screwing and unscrewing toys
dominoes
picture dominoes
figure craft
peg boards and plastic pegs
bricks (wooden and plastic), large
  and small
dolls' house (furnished)

train set
clothes-line and pegs for counting
tyres
tyre on board with castors
large circular rocker
woodwork bench with real tools
soft wood, nails
balsa wood, glue
colour matching and sorting
  material
shape-matching material
magnets
puppet theatre
puppets
washing-up bowls
dusters
scissors
pencils
Chubbi crayons and outsize
  polythene
mugs to hold crayons
scone-cutters (for plasticine)
tapwater paste
flour
salt

Toys and bought material (cont.)

marvin medium (Margros)
Cowgum
paste brushes and polythene knife-
    box to hold paste brushes
plastic spreaders
paint brushes size 10, 12
paint brushes 1 in., 2 in., 3 in., 4 in.
powder paint
mixed poster paint (gum-based)
finger-mix paint
Plasticine
clay
polythene sheeting (floor
    protection)
chalks and rubbers
paint easels
non-spill polythene paint and water
    pots

waterproof aprons
Fablon
Shireseal (for book coverings)
    tie-and-dye materials
Fabricrayons
cookery materials – aprons
    bowls
    wooden spoons
    spoons
    baking tins
    cutters
    cooling trays
Glitter dust
Polyfilla
chicken wire
polythene laundry baskets as
    containers

Dressing-up area

mirror
masks
fireman's hats (real)
nurse's outfit (First-aid materials
    and stethoscope)
bride's wear
shawls
nylon curtains
nylon nightdresses
petticoats
shirts
cloaks
dresses

skirts
nylon overalls
Indian headbands (feathered)
necklaces
bracelets
rings
scarves
belts
handbags
plastic shoe-tidies (to hold small
    articles)
pieces of fur (e.g. coat collars)

Music area

piano
recorder
tape-recorder and tapes
castanets
guitar
triangles
tambourines
drums and sticks
shakers, with sand

shakers with peas
   with stones
   with macaroni
tins with sand, gravel, peas, stones
shakers, with beer-bottle tops
record-player and records
radio
graters – 2 sticks and sandpaper
bells

Home corner

house with curtains (one-side
   pegboard for decoration)
toy cooker with graded pans
dolls' cots
different-sized dolls, black and
   white
tables, stools
tea-sets
plastic cutlery
prams
push-chairs
dolls' clothes (washable)
soft toys (washable)

bed covers (washable)
kettle
baskets
handbags
purses
plastic money
toy clock
rugs
toy sweeper
long-handled brush and dust-pan
toy telephone
feather duster
dusters

Book corner

carpeted areas with stools, chairs,
   cushions
bookcases
bookshelves
picture books
story books

scrap books
catalogues; e.g. furniture, clothes,
   seeds, etc.
home-made books (see Chapter 3)
pencils, crayons and paper

Colour-table

e.g. red one week, green another week, etc.
articles sorted by children and arranged on the table, e.g. dress, shoes, material,
   buttons, paper

Climbing

climbing frame – for indoors or
   outdoors
slides
large leather-topped stools

hollow steps
nesting boxes
metal climbing frame

Paper

kitchen paper 20 in × 30 in.
sugar paper, coloured 20 × 30 in.
coloured card (6 sheet) 20 × 30 in.
frieze paper, poster, roll 30 in. wide
coloured tissue paper
white tissue paper
sweet wrappings
biscuit wrappers
biscuit wrappings from inside tins of
   biscuits
sugar bags
kitchen foil
corrugated card from parcels
brown paper
crêpe paper

newspapers
newsprint
wallpaper sample books
odd lengths of wallpaper
toilet paper
confetti
doyleys
cellophane wrappings
bun-packets
jelly containers
silver paper
greaseproof paper
gummed paper squares, 6 in. and 8
   in., for cutting or tearing and
   sticking

Waste materials

Smarties tubes and plastic tops
cartons, e.g. cereal,
string

bottle-tops
toothpaste-tube tops
egg cartons, card and plastic

Waste materials (cont.)

straws
straw
wood shavings
sawdust
sponges
sequins
beads
macaroni, peas, beans, lentils, rice,
    spaghetti, pasta
melon seeds, orange and apple pips
potatoes (for stamping)
packing materials
polystyrene packings from parcels
polystyrene meat and vegetable
    containers
foil containers
yoghourt cartons
toilet roll middles
kitchen foil middles
scrap materials from dressmaking

or home-decorating
paper plates
egg-shells
packing cases, e.g. from TV or
    refrigerator
netting from vegetable packs
margarine containers
nylon tights and stockings
feathers
twigs
foam-rubber pieces
typewriter spools
bobbins
buttons
fathers' shirts (to wear for painting)
magazines and catalogues to cut up
    or tear
leaves
dried seaweed

Sand play

indoor tray
outdoor tray
rakes
spades
scoops
moulds
sieves
different-shaped containers, e.g.
    beakers
mugs, egg-cups

different-sized spoons
wooden spoons
sand combs
dry sand
wet sand
assorted buckets
small brushes and dustpans – for
    tidying
long-handled broom (child's)

Water play

water trough
baby bath
rubber tubing
plastic tubing
funnels
sieves
graduated beakers

sponges
plastic lids, e.g. from hair-spray
boats
soap bubbles
waterproof aprons
polythene jugs
squeezy bottles

Natural science

plants and flowers
miniature garden – indoor
shells
driftwood
stones
pebbles
smooth sea-washed glass
fish
tadpoles
guineapig
gerbils (better than hamsters
    because they are less nocturnal)
rabbit
snails
wormery

budgie
dried flower-heads and grasses
fir-cones
acorns
conkers
growing carrot-tops, turnip-tops,
    peas, beans, mustard and cress
    bulbs in season
pips growing – apple, orange, lemon
    and grapefruit
nasturtium, honesty and tomato
    seeds planted out of doors
things that float
things that sink

Outside play

balls—various sizes
hoops
rubber rings
bean bags
bat and ball
skipping-ropes
tyres

swing
roundabout
bicycle
rocking-boat
wheelbarrows
tractors
pull-along toys

Outside play (cont.)

see-saw
lorries—to sit on and push
wigwam
sand
dog on wheels
planks
prams

three-sided clothes-horse
blankets
Dandycord rugs
rubber mats
tent
groundsheet
lightweight wooden blocks (large)

Domestic materials

electric cooker
electric iron
ironing-board
Hotpoint washer with electric
   wringer
electric drying cabinet
outside drying area, with clothes-
   line and pegs
small beds with washable canvas
   base
sheets
pillow and covers
blankets
individual towels

individual face-cloths
individual combs
mops
buckets
beakers
floor-cloths
plastic sheeting (floor protection)
sweeping brushes and shovels
dustpan and hand brush
plastic tablecloths
dish-cloths
tea-towels
detergent, soap, disinfectant, bleach

Furniture

Formica-topped table (surface can
   be used for finger-painting)
stacking-chairs   ⎫
wicker armchairs   ⎬ children's size
rocking-chair   ⎭
carpets
rugs
settee—washable stretchcover

cushions for chairs
floor cushions
TV
film-projector and strips
slide-adaptor for projector
waste-bins
pedal-bin
decorated bin for odds and ends

3. Language

Educational achievement is usually measured in the medium of language. It is not surprising, therefore, that there should be a close correlation for this reason alone between deficiencies in measured ability and deficiencies in language. But the correlation is almost certainly a good deal more complex than a mere reflection of the use of verbal criteria for assessment. There is clear evidence from many sources, including such psychologists as Luria and Vygotsky, that the development and use of language contributes directly to intellectual growth.[10]

For this reason large numbers of children, probably a majority, are intellectually disadvantaged, in varying degrees, because of the poverty of their linguistic background at home. (See Chapter 4.) The Robbins Report found an inverse ratio between size of family and educational achievement.[11]

No. of children in family	Percentage of students taking degree courses
one only	13·0
two only	11·4
three only	9·0
four only	8·0
five only	3·2

Note. These are percentages when one or both parents attended a selective school. A similar inverse proportion is found when neither parent attended such a school.

No doubt there are complex reasons for this, but one may well be that the mother of the large family has to share herself and her conversation among her children. The bigger the family the less time she will devote to each one.

Dr J. W. B. Douglas has provided impressive evidence of the relationship between, on the one hand, the social class, occupations and education of the parents and, on the other, the measured ability of their children in his reports on the 1946 Cohort.[12] Here again there are a number of factors involved, but poverty of language at home certainly appears to be one of them.

The three-year-old from the working-class home mainly uses nouns, and very few descriptive words. Middle-class children use more structured language; they recall more and anticipate more. They use more qualifying parts of speech. But there are also, of course, many middle-class homes today where, because both parents work full-time or because television addiction afflicts the entire family, there is linguistic poverty. Work at the Centre for the Study of Human Development at London University has found a significant relationship between social class and verbal ability in girls at 18 months. (See page 53.)

Dr Kellmer Pringle in her studies of children in care found the same close connection between the high proportion of children who were seriously educationally backward and those with language difficulties.[13] Her evidence is particularly valuable because children who live in institutions are to some extent denied the constant dialogue with an understanding adult which is so important. It is now massively reinforced by "The Plowden Children four years later" with its clear evidence of the handicap suffered by children from working-class homes.[14] Many studies of deaf-mutes and the hard of hearing, who are the most linguistically deprived of all, notably those of Pierre Oléron in France, underline the connection.

As long ago as 1929 the Russian, Vygotsky, described the way in which young children solve the difficult problems they encounter by talking aloud about them and drawing on their previous verbal experience to find solutions. And if their verbal experience is poor and inadequate their ability to find solutions will not be very high. It is extremely important for both mothers and teachers to understand this link, not only between ability measured in verbal terms and language, and with the rat-race of eleven plus still persisting in many areas this in itself is of considerable importance, but also between intellectual growth and the development of language.

One of the most striking demonstrations of the importance of language in intellectual development has come in recent years from a class teacher in the West Riding of Yorkshire now, unfortunately, retired. Mrs Pyrah had a technique which was apparently completely simple. In her county education service it was called "asking out." She did a minimal amount of oral teaching but encouraged her children to ask the rest of the class for a solution to any problem with which they were faced. All she insisted on was that all the questions, answers and statements were framed in accurate English. It is a method which would have commended itself to Vygotsky.

Sir Alec Clegg, the Chief Education Officer, has written of her: "The reason why I think what she is doing is of such supreme importance is that I am quite convinced that children in the north of England are handicapped not by accent, not necessarily by defective grammar, but by lack of confidence which springs from the fact that they are inarticulate and know it."[15]

This method of defining each problem in accurate language, discussing it with the rest of the class and using oral language to find the answer has produced significant results in the measured ability of the children. It is further evidence of the link between the use of language and ability.

The evidence of this relationship is staring us in the face. It is no longer a hypothesis. It has been summed up by M. M. Lewis, quoted by Professor Eric Hawkins in an address to the BMA: "A fundamental factor in both cognitive and orectic (emotional) growth is the constant and permeative effect of language."[10] It is also the means by which the experience of one generation is transmitted to the next. Without it there could be no civilization.

In the first few months of life the child's brain gradually becomes aware of the fact that some sensations which come to him from the great jumble of light, sound, smell and taste which surrounds him, by way of his eyes, ears, mouth, nose or hands, occur over and over again. This recognition of a repeated signal by way of his senses is the first major step in intellectual growth. Gradually he abstracts something from each impression, e.g. from the sight, sound, smell and touch of a dog. He assembles these abstracts into a "concept" of "dog." Once the loose concept of "dog" has developed new impressions of anything remotely resembling a dog will be fitted into it, often quite inaccurately, e.g. a rabbit or a cat. These early concepts will be diffuse and ill-defined. But eventually he will begin to *define* them more accurately, indeed education, even at school and university, is to a considerable extent really only a matter of acquiring and accurately defining concepts, of organizing one's knowledge of the world into categories.

The baby will give his early concept names which may bear little resemblance to their real names, and the attaching of a name is the first big step towards more accurate definition. Michael called any fruit resembling a strawberry a "dorgy." This was the first category of things to which he gave a name.

Eventually the baby comes to know that his family also have categories of things to which they give names, which he begins to learn, e.g. book, chair, toy. He uses these names as sentences. "Book-book-book!" may mean "Give me a book," or "Here is a book."

From the naming of categories and use of one word sentences he progresses to the definition of relationships in space by the use of prepositions—"Book *on* table." This space-relationship is followed by the time-relationship with the introduction of tense: "Book was on table."

There is a great deal of controversy in linguistic research about how a child's command of syntax is acquired, and there are a number of theories about it. But clearly in forming his early sentences the young child must make choices from his vocabulary at, possibly, a number of points. The richness of the choice available to him will depend upon the names and concepts he has acquired and the practice he has had in using them. These, in their turn, will depend upon the amount and quality of language to which he has been exposed in his home, in particular on how much his mother has talked to him from his birth onwards.

It is not only the development of syntax which is obscure, but the whole process of language acquisition and, indeed, the child's motivation in learning to talk. Professor Eric Hawkins has put forward the thesis that, contrary to the popular view, the desire to communicate with mother is not the original motivation, but that language, like play, make-believe or ritual, emerges at a stage in the child's development which is predominantly concerned with symbols.[10] Its origin is in the mysterious phenomenon of play with which it is inseparately connected. Beginning as a symbolic activity, language only later takes on its powerful role as a more effective means of communication.

The gradual genesis of language from the crying of the new baby to the apparent maturity of speech of the five-year-old may be summarized thus: jargon at eighteen months, words at two, sentences at three, questions at four.

The following stages, like the norms in Chapter 1, are based upon the work of Arnold Gesell,[5] but as in the case of physical and emotional development, there are the widest differences in the times at which individual children reach the various stages. In the first few weeks of life the baby can cry but makes no other sound. By four months he can make an attractive variety of chuckles and gurgles. Three months later his sounds will include a mixture of all the vowels and most of the consonants. At ten months he responds to his name and to one or two other words. His own vocabulary will have two or three words.

The one-year-old will be responding to and communicating with his mother fairly efficiently by gestures, squeals and some words. He will be able to imitate words which are frequently repeated, and he will have added a few words to his vocabulary. He will listen to conversation.

At eighteen months he will be able to say about ten words and will be able to communicate better, often using the word as well as the gesture to do so. His baby cooing and crowing will have been replaced by the enchanting flow of jargon. He will now be able to obey one or two simple commands and he will recognize pictures, although he will not be able to name them. He will give the impression of understanding a good deal more about them than he says. As his mother names the objects in them, he will begin to learn the names and eventually point to them. A drawing on a page becomes associated with the sound of the word, e.g. "mouse," although he will probably never have seen a mouse. This is the first step towards the association of written symbols with sounds or numbers which he will acquire three or four years later—towards the threshold of literacy and numeracy.

Two is an important stage, for in the previous six months he will have acquired a few hundred words which will now replace the attractive jargon at which he was so fluent at eighteen months. He will begin to use pronouns, usually in the order "mine," "me," "you," "I," but of course he will frequently say "Michael [not "I"] sit down." In doing things he will soliloquize a great deal about what he is doing, frequently in a repetititive sing-song chant. Although we do not really understand why he does this, it is apparently important in mastering the construction of speech. At this age he loves to listen to language—particularly to simple stories about himself—about how his mother put on his clothes, made his breakfast, took him to the shops and to meet Daddy, etc. This kind of story is important in learning the meaning of words because, as his mother tells each incident, he re-lives it. He probably does not yet understand tense. His greatest intellectual achievement to date will be to recognize a word which does *not* fit an object—i.e. to make a negative judgment.

A year later he has made enormous progress. As language grows and facility in its use is improved he becomes almost a different person. One is tempted to point to this rapid transformation as evidence of the effect of language on intellectual development. It would be equally credible to regard it as the influence of intellectual growth on the development of language. Which is the chicken and which the egg is unimportant. What is clear and important is that the two are inseparable and affect each other.

By three his vocabulary may have over 1000 words. He will now use words freely to name and distinguish concepts. His soliloquizing of a year ago will have developed into dramatic play about familiar things. This play is a verbalized, dramatized thinking which is nature's own mechanism of acquiring language. He is using drama to improve his talking and from it he will learn words, phrases and syntax. He will now also be starting his career as an inveterate questioner—a period which may well drive his mother or his teacher up the wall. At this age he will often ask questions to which he knows the answers! At three, framing the question is more important to him than hearing the answer, but it should never be ignored.

At four, his questioning is almost unceasing—and he is still not very interested in the answers. What does interest him is how the answers fit in with his thoughts, with the way in which he has arranged his experience to date. His questions are asked not because he wants to know, but because they improve his ability to put his thoughts into words. Some of his questions are nothing more than thinking aloud. Although he will now begin to show clear signs of rational thought, and, indeed the beginning of an ability to think in the abstract, his stories will have a carefree mix of fact and fiction, between which he is quite unable to distinguish. This is a perfectly natural phase in his development and to exert pressure on him to "tell the truth" would be very harmful. Anyhow, what is true to him? He will probably be able to say about one thousand five hundred words, but of course they will not all be of equal importance to him.

At the end of the pre-school period he appears to his mother almost to be grown up, especially if he is her first child. She is astonished at what has become of her baby! But the air of apparent maturity which his command of language gives him is highly deceptive, covering as it does a degree of intellectual development which is still little more than rudimentary. His questioning is now a good deal less than a year ago, and its purpose now is usually to obtain information and not merely to practise his language.

He is intensely interested in the practicalities of everyday life, and his dramatic play will be concerned with the home, the shop, the hospital, the park, the street, etc.—indeed for some unknown developmental reason his imagination will be much more concerned with objective reality than it was a little while ago, or than it will be a few years later. He will not have much patience with the fairy story. His vocabulary will now have over two thousand words, and his language will be structured in more or less correct sentences.

Throughout the five years of development from the crying baby to the word-perfect five-year-old, the quality of the language element in his environment is of fundamental importance. To take the extreme case, if he heard no speech at all he would not learn to speak. Similarly the amount, variety and richness of the speech he does hear, determine the quality of his own language and have an important bearing on his intellectual growth.

Conversation with someone he loves and in whom he has confidence, someone he can call his own, is one of the major needs of the pre-school child throughout the whole period. It is also a need which makes the greatest demand on his mother or his teacher in particular, but also on his whole family. The newly born baby needs to be talked to throughout babyhood and into early infancy as part of the close, loving relationship with his mother. As early as the third or fourth month he will obviously listen and become increasingly sensitive to different tones of voice. Soft encouraging tones rather than harsh "telling-off" ones are desirable. It is also important to avoid the ridiculous baby-talk which so many parents and fond relatives still adopt in the mistaken view that they are helping their children. The baby-talk is often more difficult than the correct words. Of course he will invent his own words but parents should neither adopt these nor correct them, but continue to use the correct ones.

He will very quickly come to understand a great deal of what is said to him long before he can talk himself. His understanding will at first not be of individual words, but of the total situation to which they refer. The high degree of communication between him and his mother will rely partly on gesture, partly on tone of voice and partly on speech. At eighteen months there can be delightful conversations—mother using correct words and sentences, baby using his fluent jargon—and each knowing broadly what the other is saying. It is at this stage that his ability to articulate sounds which has emerged as part of his symbolic play starts to be used by him as a means of communication. And its effectiveness as an additional way in which he can communicate with his mother is a great motivation to learn to speak. Hence the importance of joining in the jargon conversations.

As he begins to talk the mother's conversation should always try to enlarge his vocabulary and improve his use of words, but not by directly setting out to teach him! Naming his clothes and the parts of his body as he is being dressed is a good example of how this can be done—not didactically but quietly, naturally and repetitively. Young children delight in repetition. Using simple sentences to describe what she or he is doing is another. "Mammy washes her hands" or "Michael builds a house." Speaking in sentences is very important.

His play, in a great deal of which mother will also be involved, offers constant opportunity for talk and vocabulary enrichment. But the warning in the last chapter is worth repeating. If play is overtly exploited by mothers or teachers for direct teaching purposes its educational potential will be destroyed.

One of the most trying tasks of both mother and teacher is to respond to the incessant questioning which really gets under way at three, reaches its peak at four, and falls to a more tolerable level at five. But the pre-school child's questioning is a vital stage in his intellectual development. He learns a great deal from it but, even more important, from mastering the difficult task of putting his thoughts into words. The adults surrounding him can do him no greater disservice than to ignore his questions or lose patience with them. His capacity for rational thought later in life may to a significant extent be determined by the kind of response, or lack of response, his questioning evokes from three to five.

Books also, as well as speech, play an increasingly important role from about two years of age onwards in his linguistic environment. His later education in school and college will rely heavily on them and necessarily so if education is to fulfil one of its major purposes of transmitting the accumulated knowledge of society to each succeeding generation. Because of this it is important that in the pre-school period he should become familiar with them, fond of them, aware that they contain symbols which unlock an enthralling new world. And children love symbols. This is the greatest contribution the mother, the nursery school or the playgroup can make to their children's readiness to learn to read. An absorbing interest in books and the mysteries they contain is the best impetus of all to learning to read, indeed because of it some pre-school children teach themselves to read a year before they enter the Infant School. But it cannot be over-emphasized that it is not the job of the nursery school or playgroup to teach children to read. But it certainly is their job to lead them to the point where they are dying to read. Of course the child who goes beyond this and actually reads in the nursery school should not be held back or discouraged. The occasional reader, provided he is not held up as a paragon who has beaten everyone else, will encourage the rest to reach the "readiness for reading" stage. In current discussions about methods of teaching reading we so often lose sight of what is a great deal more important than this method or that—the motivation to read. Pre-school education is concerned with motivation.

Many teachers take a familiarity with books for granted because they themselves have come from backgrounds where literacy and its trappings are commonplace. But the Plowden Report survey estimated that 29 per cent of all homes had five books or less.[16] If this is accurate, vast numbers of our children have had very little contact with books before they enter the Infant School. Many may never have handled one and some may never have seen one. In a great many homes the book represents an alien culture. This is part of the enormous initial handicap from which so many of our children never recover.

Every child should have access to attractive books from the age of two onwards. At that age a book of clear, large natural pictures of objects within his own experience will interest him. Shortly after the age of two Michael appropriated for himself a Country Life book of pictures of Britain, and by the age of three he could recognize every picture. But his favourite picture was cut out of a magazine.

As soon as he begins to talk he should also have illustrated story books available from which mother will read to him. And of course he will want the same story read over and over again. He will then "read" it himself—word perfect with the book upside down and open at the wrong page! There is a great variety of books available for the under-fives but some are quite unsuitable. Perhaps the most important requirement is that they should be about people, animals and things within their own experience. So often books for young children are either written about life in well-to-do middle-class families, which is almost completely unintelligible to most of our children, or about a soppy never-never land which is equally remote. They do indeed too often represent an alien culture. No one wants to impose the kitchen-sink syndrome on our nursery school literature, but we do want it to be about the world in which their children live and, indeed, there has been a welcome change in this direction in recent years. A major contribution to this change has been made by Leila Berg whose "Nipper" series brought a gale of fresh air into nursery education. Some of her stories are about working-class families where everything in the garden is far from lovely. And how otherwise can most of our children come to feel that books have any relevance to *them* and *their* lives and that they are not the symbols and instruments of an alien culture?

A second requirement is that fantasy should not predominate. The two-to-five age-group is passionately fond of stories about things, people and places, like those they know, e.g. "Little Peter" by Leila Berg. They also like a certain amount of magic—after all they are magicians themselves at this age and magic is real to them. They will take talking animals (such as Three Little Pigs and The Three Bears) in their stride, but many teachers seem agreed that the books of Beatrix Potter have little appeal for most children today. It is difficult to understand why this is so. The kind of animals which attract them most varies from one area to another. The headmistress of an Infant School at Featherstone, West Riding, said that hers was a dog area. Some areas are dog areas, while others are cat, sheep or cow areas. The lurid stories of cunning witches, voracious dragons and wicked giants are quite unsuitable and may indeed be harmful—leading to unnecessary fears and nightmares.

Apart from this, it cannot be over-emphasized that young children love best of all books about young children just like themselves and about the simple, familiar aspects of their everyday lives. The books most frequently purchased by parents are the Ladybird books of which at the time of writing there are over 260 titles. One important rule for parents buying books is that it is usually unwise to buy those in use at the Infant School to which their children will go. Teachers are generally willing to give advice to mothers about suitable books—indeed at some schools there is a bookshop for parents, e.g. at the Montem Infants' School in London.

Apart from books of stories which can be read to them, young children should have available a variety of books. Every nursery class and playgroup, as well as every home, should have a collection—a book corner, a nursery library. The books should be of various sizes and weights, and with attractive jackets. They should be mainly of pictures, both photographs and line drawings. Many teachers say they find the books illustrated by Brian Wildsmith particularly attractive to their children. They should also contain words, but not too many, which children from about two and a half will pretend to read. For this reason the layout of the book is important. It should be simple and clear with good type. This will encourage word recognition during "pretending" reading. The shoddy book with fussy, tasteless layout should be avoided like the plague—as should the dog-eared grubby pile of comics so often seen in playgroups and some nursery classes.

Some of the most valuable nursery library books of all are those made by mother or teacher and the children themselves. Books of their own paintings are a constant source of interest. Perhaps the most important pre-reading task is to convince children that books are a vast source of interest, and their own art is always interesting to them. Bound collections of pictures of school or home activities are a perennial source of interest e.g. shopping, the kitchen, the garden, the nature table, birds, flowers, insects, etc.

If all our children could be surrounded with attractive books to which they had completely free access from the age of two onwards how many problems of illiteracy would vanish! It is of course important that the mother or the teacher should display an equal interest in them with their children. Looking at books will be an adult interest they will want to share. The three-year-olds will ask what the words below the pictures say and they should then, and only then, be told. If attempts are made to teach them to read the words before they really want to do so, they may be put off books for life.

The young child will pretend to read words and may learn to recognize some, indeed he may learn to read, and his approach to the concept of a symbol on a page representing a thing, an action, a quantity, may be by way of books. But the use of a symbol to represent his ideas, thoughts or feelings will usually be by way of his hands—by the mastery of the crayon, the pencil and the paintbrush. As he explores and masters a medium his efforts will begin to reflect his feelings. At first he will cover page after page with one colour, but his choice of colour will come to be determined by whether he feels happy and secure when it will be bright, or unhappy and insecure when it will be dark. This use of colour, which may be at about the age of twenty-four to thirty months, is the first step in visual representation on paper of something within himself which he wishes to communicate, record, or even merely express.

After the pages of plain colour he may, for a time, be more attracted to painting himself—his hands or face. This is a passing phase, and he will soon return to paper, for which his teacher will be very thankful. When he does so there will be clear but embryonic signs of form emerging in his paintings. At first these will be circular or grid patterns. More often than not he will end up by covering these first ventures into form by the sheet of plain colour which occupied him a few months earlier. Eva Frommer has found in her clinical work that this stage of emerging form often coincides with the beginning of word formation and with sphincter control.[17]

Slowly, form appears more clearly in his paintings and drawings and he begins to identify things although the form will not remotely resemble them in adult reality. This wiggle is a cat and that blob a man. But, to him, they are real enough. It is of the utmost importance to his eventual readiness to read that the adults around him should take these pictures as seriously as he does. After all, the word "dog" which mother reads looks even less like a dog than his drawing of one! And why should his symbol not command as much respect as hers?

Provided his efforts have had the generous and sympathetic response they deserve, he will more and more produce drawings which, while far from accurate representations, possess the essential quality of the thing he is putting on paper. Michael's drawings of an elephant at three were unlike any elephant which ever lived, but they had an unmistakable "elephantness" which is the glory of children's art. And does the warning need repeating?—never, never, never try to teach the pre-school child, or any young child, to draw. Give him the tools, interest and encouragement and leave his spontaneity free to roam where and how it will. In his own good time, and it will come much quicker if he is left free, he will conform to recognized and recognizable methods of drawing houses, men and dogs. When this happens and he has learnt how to represent people, things and even feelings on paper, he is ready to take the next step which man took in the forward march of civilization, instead of drawing the thing itself, as in Egyptian hieroglyphics, to represent it by a symbol called a word.

It is not the task of pre-school education to teach children to write but, as in the case of reading, it is its job to bring them to the threshold of writing by the sensitive handling of their exploration of paint and crayon. But, again as with reading, if a child does begin to write in the pre-school years he should not be stopped. Encouragement should be in a low key in case it dissipates the desire to learn, and every teacher is familiar with the child whose will to learn has been stifled by over-keen parents.

In the all-important field of language development the task of the play group or nursery school can be summarized under three headings. First, it should provide a language-rich environment in which the pre-school child, particularly if he comes from an inarticulate home, can increase his vocabulary of nouns and verbs but, more important, of qualifying words, and gain confidence in structuring his language. Second, by familiarizing him with books, creating an interest in them and in the interesting world they can reveal, it should bring him to the point where he is ready and anxious to learn how to unlock the mysteries for himself. Third, by providing opportunity and materials it can encourage him to express himself, his ideas and concepts as well as his feelings, on paper. In short, its function is to enable him to come to the threshold of literacy with an urge to step over it which is so strong that it will not be denied.

4. Deprivation

The term "deprivation" when applied to children usually includes three groups—those in care, those who are in their own homes but suffer emotional deprivation because they are unloved and rejected, and those whose homes are culturally and educationally unstimulating. In this book the term is used more widely, to include children who suffer from the effects of nutritional and general baby-rearing deficiencies.

The earliest requirement of the unborn baby are for adequate nutrition, freedom from the harmful effects of excessive smoking or drug taking by the mother, from illnesses such as rubella and abnormal physical or emotional disturbances.

By the twenty-fifth week of gestation the unborn baby's brain has achieved its adult number of unit cells, which cannot multiply and are incapable of repair afterwards. Following this, from about the thirtieth week up to the first few months of post-natal life there is a considerable burst of brain growth, of nerve fibres growing out of the established nerve cells, of the connections between them, of cells concerned with myelin and of the process of myelination (i.e. the ensheathing of cells). It is during this period of most rapid growth of the content of the brain that babies are at their most vulnerable. Maximum growth is accompanied by maximum risk.

Dr John Dobbing has described experiments on animals showing the persisting deficits in brain development and functioning caused by under-nutrition during this spurt period in growth.[18] Brain weight was permanently less, there were 10–20 per cent fewer brain cells and the degree of myelination was less. The cerebellum, where the concentration of cells is greatest, was the most seriously affected part and there was detectable impairment of cerebellar functions such as the finer motor co-ordinations. There is a high degree of probability that similar damage is caused by under-nutrition in the case of babies. If growth is

49

retarded by under-nutrition or for any other reason during the gestation period, particularly the latter part of it, or in the early months of infancy, there does appear to be a danger of permanent brain impairment.

Professor J. McKeown found a correlation between birth-weight and verbal reasoning scores in the eleven-plus selection examinations.[19] In a report by the National Children's Bureau edited by Dr Kellmer Pringle studies are described which show that low birth-weight for gestational age is associated with later educational backwardness, with minor disabilities such as clumsiness and poor adjustment and also with more serious handicaps and abnormalities.[20] There is also accumulating evidence that children with low birth-weight are particularly vulnerable to poor environments.

Of course low birth-weight may be associated with factors such as short stature of parents or excessive smoking by the mother during pregnancy, and there is a correlation with social class. Nevertheless there is little doubt that it is often a result of dietary deficiencies. Dr Dobbing, in his paper, estimated that one-third of babies of low birth-weight for their gestational age suffered from retarded intra-uterine growth.

Professor R. S. Illingworth in an article in the *Medical News Tribune* (13 November 1972) pointed to the possibility of large amounts of drugs taken in the form of medicines obtained without prescription causing abnormalities in their unborn children. A study of women in pregnancy from three to nine weeks showed that each had taken 8·7 drugs, and that 80 per cent of them were taken without medical advice.

Professor P. E. Vernon has summarized the position as far as we know it:

"Apparently the infant brain is particularly vulnerable to dietary deficiencies during later pregnancy and early feeding, say from three months before to three months after birth. The damage occurring then to the brain cells from lack of protein, proper vitamins and other crucial elements may be irreversible; it cannot be made up even if the older infant or child is relatively well fed."[21]

In South African research which he describes children, undernourished in their first two years, were found to achieve lower scores in both verbal and non-verbal tests and, indeed, were found in their scores to resemble those of brain-damaged children.

Abnormal gestational periods extending beyond 40 ± 2 have been found to have a correlation with depressed social adjustment and reading scores at seven years of age. "In fact gestational maturity appeared to be a better predictor of reading ability and social adjustment at seven years than the more commonly accepted birth-weight measurement."[21]

It has been suggested that because of this correlation the obstetric practice of induced labour should be more widely used. At present it is mainly a convenience for well-to-do mothers. However, the abnormal gestational period itself is probably the result of other factors and not a cause of lower ability scores in the primary school child.

In his controversial paper Professor A. R. Jensen took the view that pre-natal influences were probably the major *environmental* factor in measured intelligence.[22] Perhaps the most striking evidence of the association between early and severe malnutrition and brain function has come from Dr Joaquin Cravioto of the Hospital Infantil de Mexico, who set the maximum danger period at −30 weeks to +18 months.

While the connection between under-nourishment in the few months around birth and the permanent impairment of the child's brain and consequently of his intellectual development appears now to be well established, there is still considerable scope for research—particularly into the influence of the physical state of the brain on intellectual capacity.

It appears to follow from this well-established connection that once the earliest months of life have passed and the structure of the brain and nervous system are well established, the effect of later under-nourishment, physically harmful though it will certainly be, will result in less, and ultimately in no, physical damage to the brain—though it may cause "temporary" backwardness. In adult life starvation to the point of death appears to cause no permanent brain damage. This was illustrated in many tragic cases in the Nazi concentration camps. Professor Vernon has pointed out that the minor retardation of development which often occurs at weaning may be psychological rather than a result of a change of diet.[21]

The effect of under-nourishment on intellectual development is clearly a major factor in the educational deprivation of children from poorer homes—those euphemistically called "slow learners." Their ability to learn may well be permanently depressed because of dietary deficiencies in their earliest months. This is of great importance for mothers, teachers, and, for those who are concerned with policy locally in the social service departments of local authorities and nationally where social policy such as the provision of milk in primary schools is decided. This is a time of rising living standards but of course they are unequally distributed. Nutritional standards may certainly be generally better than a generation ago, though this is not always the case. In 1971 The Child Poverty Action Group estimated that two million children were living below the level of poverty as defined in "Circumstances of Families," 1967. In a survey of the feeding habits of schoolchildren in 1970 it was found that the dietary patterns of 32 per cent qualified as satisfactory, 57 per cent unsatisfactory and 11 per cent extremely poor and there were wide regional variations. Eighteen per cent of primary and 44 per cent of secondary children were deficient of calcium and 28 per cent and 67 per cent respectively of riboflavine.[23] There is also the almost equally harmful nutritional phenomenon caused by affluence, the over-nourished child who suffers from obesity. Physical care may have improved, but little else. So far as language and general cultural standards are concerned the home may actually be more impoverished than a generation ago. Indeed the price of affluence may be largely paid by the youngest members of the family when it is obtained by mother's full-time employment. There is no connection whatever between affluence and affection and the home without love is the most deficient of all.

There are unfortunately still homes where even physical care—food, hygiene, clothing, etc.—is inadequate. This may be due to a deficiency in the mother herself or to such factors as domestic discord or acute illness in the family, particularly mental illness, or indeed to poverty. But poverty alone is rarely associated with inadequate care though, if acute, it may result in under-nutrition—an extremely serious condition with danger of permanent impairment in the case of very young children.

After birth the home environment, in particular the mother, must be relied upon to provide the appropriate stimulus at the appropriate time for the baby to develop naturally and normally. And research at Edinburgh University has shown that a baby's intellectual growth begins immediately after birth.

However, in spite of all the research into human development, the precise requirements are still largely unknown. Growth is by the building of associations of nerve cells in the brain; e.g. as the use of eyes and hand is co-ordinated. We think, but we do not know, that the strength and degree of permanence of these associations depends upon the baby's brain being stimulated at a particular time. We also believe that if these associations are formed in infancy they are more likely to endure. There is a fair degree of probability about this. But what is quite unknown to us at present is the effect on these associations in the brain of over-early stimulation—trying to teach a child something, e.g. to read, before he is ready for it—or, on the other hand, of not providing the stimulus when it appears to be needed.

However, from the norms of development described in Chapter 1 we know broadly what the physical, social and emotional requirements are throughout the pre-school period. Also, apart from the norms a number of tests have been developed for assessing a baby's development. Gesell (1947) was, of course, a pioneer in this field, but at least two systems preceded his—that of Buhler and Hetzer (1935) and of Nancy Bayley (1933). Since Gesell there have been others but the first scale specifically for British children was developed by Griffiths (1954). It consisted of five sub-scales in each of which there are 52 items: Loco-motor, Personal-Social, Hearing-Speech, Eye-Hand and Personal. The Griffiths sçales have been extremely useful in a number of ways—not least in assessing the influence of home background on development.

Work at the Centre for the Study of Human Development at London University shows that scores in these baby tests are a predictor, but a low-level one only, of later IQ. The fact that the level of prediction is a poor one before the age of three appears to indicate that in later measured ability environment plays an important part to change the earlier measurement. This is borne out by an important fact which has emerged from these studies. There was found to be a significant relationship between social class and IQ from three years of age onwards. So far as verbal ability alone was concerned there was found to be by eighteen months an equally significant relationship with social class among girls. Verbally handicapped because of social class by eighteen months! The relationship among boys appeared later. Indeed the correlations among girls are higher at each age and this may indicate that girls are more susceptible to environmental influences than boys.

Linguistic deprivation is the commonest and intellectually most damaging deprivation of all. It may be caused by poverty of language in the home, a TV-addicted home or a home deprived of mother and father for most of the waking hours—where household chores occupy the few hours in the evening when mother is at home. Poverty of language is still associated with social class but what used to be regarded as almost exclusively a working-class deficiency is now to be found in all social strata. The working mother, TV-addiction and the broken home are to be found among all classes.

The development of language is so essential to intellectual growth that the baby needs conversation literally from birth onwards. He should be talked to a great deal more than is usual in many homes. But he should not be talked to. in baby talk—"gee-gee. moo-cow, chuck-chuck," etc.—or exclusively in nouns and verbs. At every stage in his growth he needs the stimulus of conversation, e.g. even the stage of phonetic jumble towards the end of his first year is extremely important in the emergence of language. The phonetic elements may be in a mix-up but at least he is learning them by imitation. "Just baby talk? On the contrary, only if we talk to babies will they outgrow the need for baby talk. The more children are spoken to and read to, the more readily will they learn to enjoy the give and take of conversation."[13] Without this interaction between mother and child there would be no development.

The story-telling which enthralls them from the second half of the second year and the incessant questioning which comes rather later will be equally demanding of the parents' time and patience. To listen to a baby is as important as to talk to him. In an investigation at Harvard University into all the factors which distinguish the successful mother it has been found that mothers spend less than a tenth of the child's day talking to him.

The main concentration of working-class children are in what the Newson Report called the "grey" areas and the cities of the north rather than in the counties and the county towns of the south.[24] And all too often these are the areas in which the schools are old, inadequate and understaffed. "Here education is not an opportunity but a brief and irrelevant prelude to work."[25] They tend to live in overcrowded homes, in poorer housing. They are in larger families and more of their parents left school at the statutory leaving age and are in the lowest-paid occupational groups. More working-class children are in need of special education, and the incidence of illness is higher among them than among middle-class children; e.g. bronchitis amongst miners, their wives and children is twice the national average.

"When children are poor, they are less likely to benefit from their edication. They go to poor schools in areas where they must live. They must live in them because their parents are poor. Their parents become poorer because of the area in which they live. Whole families are caught in a cat's cradle of deprivation and poverty and for many of them there is never any escape . . . . This is another poverty trap—children who are the victims of multiple poverty. They have not a chance."[26]

The effect of most of these impediments to child development related to social class has been measured, but to them could be added such factors as fewer books in the home and Plowden found that 29 per cent of homes had fewer than six;[16] shared bedrooms and beds; lack of a private place for play or, later for study; lack of interesting holidays and travel; the employment pattern of the parents.

The result of all the handicaps which flow from social class, and are largely perptuated from one generation to another, become only too obvious as soon as the baby moves from his predominantly physical environment in the eighteen months after birth to one in which cultural, and social factors increasingly influence him. After those early months social-class differences emerge in measured ability and grow into a yawning gulf in the primary and secondary school stages with the walls of the gulf moving outwards throughout school life, e.g. upper middle-class children who at eight had T scores of 56–60 had gained 1·52 points at eleven, but children in the lower working-class who had scored equally with them at eight had actually lost 2·27 points at eleven. This cumulative deterioration in the performance of working-class children relative to middle-class children whose home environment is better, which applies both to measured intelligence and school performance, means that by eleven the child of the manual worker has fallen far behind the child of middle-class parents. As a consequence Dr Douglas found that 54 per cent of upper middle-class children went to the grammar school but only 11 per cent of lower working-class children.[12]

The argument that the wide differences at eleven are largely genetic scarcely bears examination in view of the diverging graphs of children who at three, and sometimes at eight, had been equal. They point unmistakably to the child's environment, linguistic and cultural, as well as physical and emotional, as a major determinant of later ability and progress.

The effect of environment on measured ability has been illustrated in a large number of studies in many countries; for example, Burt found a correlation of 0·944 among identical twins who had been reared together, but one of 0·771 only among those who had been reared separately.

Laycock and Munro quote a number of American and Canadian studies which have reached a similar conclusion. "The child . . . creates a world of meaning out of his experiences with his own body and with the environment around him."[27] He is to a considerable extent what his environment has made him.

After adequate nutrition a young child's greatest need is for affection and the security it gives him.

From the first obvious dawn of intelligence—though its actual dawn was within days of birth—when he smiles up at his mother the baby needs much more than a nurse or minder, however skilful and dedicated the nursing or minding may be. He also needs companionship and love which is neither obsessive nor authoritarian, but understanding and loving companionship from all the members of his family. Only in this atmosphere can his socialization develop naturally and free from strain, and his identity as a person in his own right. The obsessive mother is often the one with an unsatisfactory marital relationship. She uses her child as a source of emotional satisfaction to a degree which impedes his development and she may not even be aware that she is doing so.

"Now all we know is that if children in the first two or three years get the kind of support and affection I'm referring to, then when they are three plus, they become increasingly confident and able to make use of the world as they find it, a wider world. And it's the ones who don't—who don't get what we're referring to in the first two or three years, who are apprehensive and bothered and become dependent; it's a complete paradox, you see, the complete opposite of what the popular theory of spoiling implies. No, the fact is that this growth, this change from being perhaps very clinging … a lot of mothers are terribly worried because a child of two years say three months or two years and six months, she says 'He's more clinging today that he was,' but if only they can wait till he's about two years and nine, three, three and a half, then they will find that hey presto, it's a different world."[28]

Equally inimical to his development is the home where the role of the father is unclear or where he has ceased to make a contribution to the family life. The child will build an inner world for himself without his father in it, or with him only in diffuse terms. This has been found to be a common factor among large numbers of delinquent children.

Without affection, unashamedly demonstrated, both emotional and intellectual growth will be held back.

Apart from nutritional deficiencies, those which derive from the class differential in living and cultural standards or from the inadequate mother, a child is deprived in a particularly damaging way if he lacks space in which to play or materials with which to play. Space is a baby's birthright; the lack of it is the bugbear of modern urban living. Many children in blocks of flats are virtually homebound. In high-rise living the over-anxious mother who is afraid of her child falling out of the window, down the lift-shaft or off the balcony, produces a corresponding tension in her child, who is cooped up with her all day. As he emerges from babyhood into early infancy he needs more and more space to explore—first the three dimensions of his own position in it, e.g. the space above him in his cot, when he reaches for the coloured ribbons, then the outer quality of space in the wider area he can cover as a nine-months crawler followed by the even bigger world of the toddler, including the mysterious region upstairs. Finally he explores the wider, outdoor space as a vigorous, athletic three- or four-year-old. Play space and play material are two of childhood's greatest needs. Thus the environment of babyhood and early infancy has physical, linguistic, social and emotional dimensions which are all essential and which it is primarily the function of the home to supply.

As well as the obviously deprived children mentioned above, social scientists are uncovering new categories. A recent example is the study undertaken by the National Children's Bureau of illegitimate children, which showed, in all social classes, a higher incidence of difficulties in behaviour and learning performance than among children born legitimate.[29]

In addition to all these there are probably 70,000 children in residential care. The emotional and intellectual handicap they suffer, no matter how dedicated the service of those who are responsible for them, has been investigated by Dr Kellmer Pringle and Victoria Bossio.[13]

There are a roughly similar number of children with physical handicaps whose development may be impeded unless they have special educational provision. There are also other groups at considerable risk of under-development if left entirely to the home environment; for example, immigrant children whose parents speak little or no English.

These all add up to a very great number of children in our society for whom special educational provision of one kind or another outside the home is much more than a desirable additional stimulus to that of the home, and it is almost always that, but is essential if they are to avoid a long, cummulative retardation of development. Some are handicapped at birth, or before, some shortly afterwards.

The environment, principally the home and the mother, must satisfy a number of basic needs. If they are not satisfied children suffer the deleterious effects of their deprivation. These may range from permanent physical, intellectual or emotional damage to a failure to fulfil their potential at school.

Where the environment is unsatisfactory the education system must provide a different environment which is deliberately designed to compensate for environmental handicaps. But if it is left beyond the early years the damage is irreversible. More than half of adult intelligence is acquired before a child enters the Infant School and three-quarters by the time he leaves it to go to the Junior School. The chances of success diminish, and eventually disappear as the child gets older. Indeed there appears to be a law emerging from many recent studies about the chances of success of positive action to reverse the intellectual effects of deprivation on children. The earlier in life it is suffered the more likely its influence is to be permanent and, therefore, the greater and earlier the effort needed. The longer the delay the less its chances of success. Hence the importance, the lifelong importance, of the early years before the deprivation gap becomes unbridgeable.

5. The Case

Nature clearly intended parents to bring up their own children, but the functions of parenthood appear to have developed in three stages. The earliest, seen in lower forms of animal life such as insects, was to transmit to their offspring a genetic pattern which would determine their behaviour to the end of their days. Secondly, as their young began to need a period of infant dependence, they began also to provide care and nurture for them, as long as they were dependent. Finally, in the case of human beings, the period of dependence increased, the genetic pattern became a less influential key to behaviour, and parents had also to impart the skills and knowledge necessary for survival in the physical environment.

But long, long ago, as community life developed with its codes, creeds and customs and the social environment became important the parental role had to be supplemented by the community itself and the idea of the group acting *in loco parentis* to bring up its young emerged. In primitive societies the elders of the tribe initiated the young into the customs of tribal life. In biblical times the synagogue instructed children in the Mosaic Law. In English medieval society the gild had a clearly defined educational function. As the horrors of the Industrial Revolution multiplied in the early 19th century, a whole range of schools mushroomed to educate the poor.

The more complicated society became the more it became necessary for the teaching role of the parent to be supplemented by that of the community and today, because of the sophistication of our world by the advance of science and technology, it has almost been superseded. Indeed, in some countries the community has very nearly taken over the whole task from early infancy to the end of school life—for example, the child of the Russian factory worker or of an Israeli Kibbutznik.

In most western countries there is a fairly long period of compulsory full-time education, starting usually at five or six. (See Chapter 6.) However, in recent years the period of school life has been extended at each end almost everywhere. In Britain the leaving age was raised to sixteen in 1972 but about 17·8 per cent of pupils stay at school beyond this age (Maintained Schools only, January 1971). At the other end, probably about 300,000 children below the age of five attend a maintained school or day nursery. In addition about 200,000 attend playgroups and upwards of 100,000 are cared for by child-minders. Nevertheless there is intense and growing pressure for more places for the three- and four-year-old age-groups. If provided they would involve a significant diversion of educational resources—in particular of teachers and buildings from other parts of the education system unless education was given a much bigger share of the gross domestic product. A plan for expansion to meet the probable demand is outlined and costed in Chapter 7.

Is there a case for the development of yet another sector of an already huge and costly education system to add to the present pattern of primary, secondary and tertiary, or would the resources be educationally more effective if employed in improving what we are often doing inadequately for other age-groups—for example, to make a reality of day-release for the unfortunate 16–18-year-olds who leave school at the earliest possible moment permitted by the law and have no further contact with the education system?

In the case of one category of children there can be little doubt about the answer. Chapter 4 discussed the effects of deprivation on educational achievement. The persistence of thoroughly unsatisfactory home backgrounds is known to be resulting in a colossal waste of native ability which a manufacturing country with few raw materials and dependent in the main on exploiting its ability and skill cannot afford. Apart from the economics of this waste, it is surely the birthright of every child to be given the opportunity to develop his potential to the fullest possible extent. But his environment may prevent this. His handicap may be physical, cultural, emotional or social.

But home backgrounds cannot be changed overnight, nor indeed in some respects in a generation, particularly where the problem is cultural poverty, parental attitudes or poverty of language, but at the very least we can and should begin to compensate the unfortunate children who are handicapped by them. Their difficulties are often connected with social class differentials in environment, housing, language, cultural opportunities, etc. And we must begin to break this dreary generation-to-generation chain of social-class educational handicap both by reducing these differentials and by compensating the child for their effects on him.

Plowden has been on our bookshelves for five years and still we have not to any significant extent, except in a £16 million EPA programme and the Urban Aid Programme, altered our distribution of educational resources positively to discriminate in favour of those children who for one reason or another are unable to realize their potential. As a result, we continue to allow our national army of "mute inglorious Miltons" to receive its annual increment of recruits from the secondary schools—undeveloped, unstretched, with a sense of failure which is only too obvious from the fact that three-quarters of those who leave school at the statutory age have no further contact of any kind with the education system.

Not only does this annual wastage go on year after year, but it also leads to a further waste of resources—in remedial teaching in the secondary schools. This probably accounts for 10 per cent of all teaching time. But, as survey after survey has shown, one of the latest being the NFER Report on reading standards, there has been no quantifiable improvement since 1964.[30] This should be taken into account in any attempt to assess the cost of nursery education.

If the growth of educational handicap is seen as a "V" the time to apply teaching resources to counteract it, if they are to be effective, is at the base where the gap begins to appear: i.e. about the age of three years. Left to 11-plus it will be too late for the majority of children. Translated into military terms, the application of effort where the gap first appears rather than trying to close it when it is deep and broad, is a principle of which Clausewitz himself would certainly have approved!

Amosov has said that one extra year at the bottom of the scholastic ladder is worth two at the top. And the old Jesuit maxim is equally true: "Give me a child until he is seven and I will give you the man." Wordsworth made the same point—"The child is father of the man." We are what we are largely because of what happened to us in the earliest years of our lives. After that the pattern is set and more difficult to change.

For children who for one reason or another are deprived by their circumstances pre-school education is essential. There can be no doubt about this. And the present provision for them is hopelessly inadequate. Indeed, if all the present places in maintained schools were filled by deprived children, and they are probably in a minority in the schools at present, they would still be insufficient.

But what about the children outside this category? Is there a case for providing for them also? About some of them, again there can be little doubt. They are the children of mothers who are forced by economic circumstances to take full-time jobs. They may be unmarried mothers, divorced or separated, or have low-paid husbands. It is difficult to estimate the number of mothers who fall into this category. 43·5 per cent of married women undertook full-time employment, or sought it, in 1971, but for many it was not essential to do so, and many had no children. It was estimated by NEDO in 1972 that three million men earned less than £20 per week, but not all were married, and of those who were some had no children. Again there were 89,000 divorces in 1971 and 65,000 illegitimate births. All the factors which go to making up this category of parents point to a considerable and growing number of children for whom day provision of some kind is needed, and as they are deprived of parental influence for some hours each day, the day care should have an educational content. This is a second category for whom nursery education is necessary and, in this case, there is a direct and measurable economic return from the work which the mother is able to undertake, but, from the children's point of view, there is an additional benefit in the improvement which the mother's income will normally make to the physical quality of the home. Standard of living is an important factor in determining whether or not a child fulfils his potential. In a great many single-parent families there is also a good deal to be said for giving the mother a few hours each day away from her children. The widow or unmarried mother often has no other relief.

However, probably the majority of our young children are neither deprived nor have mothers who must go out to work. Is there a case for providing nursery places for this more fortunate group? One of the problems about answering this question is that there is little positive evidence yet that children who have pre-school education derive any lasting educational benefit from it. Dr Halsey's recent report provides some evidence that they have an advantage in the Infant School.[31]

No statistically reliable or significant data is available about the long-term effects of pre-school education because at present it is available to so few, and of these a high proportion have been given places entirely for social reasons. Most of the evidence to support the universal provision of nursery schools is negative. However, there is overwhelming evidence and agreement on the importance of the pre-school *years* in deciding whether or not a child develops his genetic potential to the optimum.

Because of this lack of evidence the Plowden Report based its support for pre-school education on the ". . . overwhelming evidence of experienced educators."[16] And this was a sensible thing to do. To this one might add the enthusiastic support of parents. At a typical Tyneside Infant School with a nursery class there is a long waiting-list for the thirty places available. It is common for mothers of young babies to enter their names! The famous public schools now share this distinction with the nursery schools. The parents are required to state their reasons for wanting their children to be admitted. An analysis of the present waiting lists shows the following order of priorities:

	Reasons	*Times given (percentage)*
1	Needs other children to play with	45
2	Can't let him out to play because of busy road	17
3	Mother wants to work	9
4	Preparation for school	8
5	Illness of mother	4
	Language problems	4
6	Needs to be occupied and can't devote sufficient time to him	3
	Cries when older brothers and sisters go to school	3
7	Miscellaneous	7

The majority are not educational reasons, but this is understandable because the small number of places available to serve a catchment area which provides an annual intake of 120 children to the Infant School inevitably means that non-educational criteria are used by the headmistress in allocating places.

The small survey referred to on page 1, also made in a working-class area of Tyneside, gives a different picture.[1]

This does appear to show that contrary to popular belief working-class parents really do believe in nursery education and want it for their children.

	Replies of mothers (percentage)	
A child who has been to nursery school has an advantage over children who have not.	Agree	78
	Disagree	16
	Don't know	6
A nursery school gives a child a good start in life.	Agree	77
	Disagree	10
	Don't know	13
There isn't much a child can get from a nursery school which it can't get from its own mother.	Agree	20
	Disagree	66
	Don't know	14
All parents who wish to send their children to state nursery schools between the ages of 3 and 5 should be able to do so.	Agree	96
	Disagree	3
	Don't know	1
The main value of nursery schools is that they help mothers who have to go out to work.	Agree	62
	Disagree	35
	Don't know	3
Nursery schools are necessary for children from broken homes but not for children from happy families.	Agree	11
	Disagree	83
	Don't know	6
A child who has been to school before the age of five is more likely to do well at school later on.	Agree	47
	Disagree	40
	Don't know	13
Nursery schools might do some children good, but I doubt whether my own little boy/girl would gain much from going to one.	Agree	26
	Disagree	66
	Don't know	8

The Plowden Report said there were educational, social, health and welfare benefits to be gained from nursery schools.[16] The Council for Educational Advance in a recent Nursery School Campaign pamphlet stated the case in this way:

"Space and opportunity for play are essential for the normal development of children. Satisfactory play has the same beneficient effect as sunshine and fresh air. It is health-giving in some mysterious way of its own, and to be provided with the right opportunity for it is as important to the child as is food and shelter.

"In a nursery school or class, under the guidance of qualified teachers and assistants, a child has opportunity to make his own discoveries in an environment which is specially planned for him. He can touch and handle everything within reach. He can experiment with basic things like sand, clay, water, earth and paint, and discover for himself what they will do, what control he has over them.

"He delights in developing his physical skill, in running, balancing and climbing. To do this in company with others adds to his pleasure and satisfaction. He extends his understanding by his imaginative play. He gradually learns to do things with others, and the self-discipline involved in 'taking turns.' A vital part of all this experience is talk, and his growing ability to listen and to communicate. It is his first adventure out from his home, and usually a half-day session for the three- and four-year-olds is enough.

"If he can have this kind of experience in the pre-school years, how much better equipped he will be to profit from all that the primary school will offer him later on."

O. M. Woodward of the Froebel Educational Institute summarized the case thus:[32]

"The Nursery School is no longer a place where children can be dumped while their mothers go out to work, or a place where the deficiencies in a child's physical development, only, are made good. The aim now is to help the child in his all-round development, to *supplement* the home, but not to *substitute* for it. Therefore the Nursery School takes into account his social development; it attempts to help him to control his strong aggressive impulses or to cease to be over-submissive, cowed and frightened. It tries to give him the widest possible range of experiences so that his intellectual ability will develop; it attempts to surround him with as much beauty both natural and man-made as possible, so that he may develop aesthetically and spiritually, and it attempts to help him to develop physically as fully as possible."

In stating the case for nursery education for all children, not merely the deprived or those whose mothers must work, four points need emphasis. First, by far the greatest merit of the nursery class or the playgroup is that it gives to almost all children considerably greater scope for play. Play is nature's teacher and without space and materials for it a young child cannot develop intellectually, socially, or physically. Modern urban living rarely makes sufficient provision for the very young child. Particularly hard-hit are the flat-dwellers whose young children can only go out of doors when Mum takes them. The older children can go to the park or play in the street, but the three- or four-year-olds are almost permanently confined to a 150 sq ft living room, three-quarters of which will be occupied with furniture, and a tiny kitchen. A typical remark made by a mother on the application forms mentioned on page 65 is: "Richard is not allowed to play outside the house as we live on a main bus route." If Mum is houseproud, as she often is today, and cannot live with a permanent clutter of toys on the floor, her child really belongs to the deprived category. Play to a young child is as important as hygiene and intellectually a good deal more important.

The nursery class or playgroup has, or should have, adequate space for play both indoors and outdoors. The Department of Education and Science have quite strict regulations about the floor space which must be available per child. (See Chapter 8.) The nursery class also has a rich variety of play material. The list given in Chapter 2 of the material available in a typical nursery class shows the great range of both commercially produced and improvised materials—a wonderland of toys, paint, sand, water, bricks, pets, books, etc., where the three-year-old can experiment and experience to his heart's content.

The physical aspect of play is also important at three. It is the age when massive muscular activity and the performing of physical feats, often hair-raising to the mother, is important in his development. The well-equipped nursery provides for this phase.

A second essential need of the young child, if he is to reach his potential in the education system, is the opportunity to talk a great deal and hear others talk. The connection between growth of language and intellectual development was mentioned in Chapter 3. It is not just a matter of learning to communicate with others—though that is extremely important—but of the development of the ability to think and reason. One of the problems at this age is that perceptual as well as conceptual development is very often ahead of vocabulary. Without language to enable him to arrange his growing inner model of the world around him, the three-year-old is at a considerable disadvantage.

The modern nursery school is as rich in spoken language—teachers', nursery assistants', other children's, radio and television—as it is in play material. In it there is far more opportunity to acquire both vocabulary and syntax, than in the home. It gives the child opportunity to indulge in chanting and repetition, which he loves, and to dramatize his play, which he must do to get the maximum benefit from it. In addition he becomes familiar with, and intensely interested in, the symbolism of words. It is the task of pre-school education to bring him to the threshold of reading, with eager expectation, and through his exploration of the media, of writing also. To create this linguistic environment requires skill and training which the teacher and trained playgroup leader possess.

The context for play and through it learning of many kinds, and for the growth of language, cannot be provided even in the best home in the rich and expert way in which it can in the nursery class.

Thirdly, nursery education is about confidence and personal identity. The home can never provide enough young children to enable its own children to become confident in society. The average family size today is 2·97. And saying they are confident in society means they have found their own identity. To find their own identity is to acquire confidence generally. Many teachers regard the acquiring of confidence as the chief merit of nursery education.

Confidence is closely related to attitude towards school. The free, caring atmosphere of the nursery class with its vast amount of exciting material, will be an attractive place—far removed from the usual connotation of "school" which may have been imparted by parents or older brothers and sisters. Too often the school is regarded as the alien culture referred to on page 43. But to the child from the nursery, the Infant School will be anticipated keenly as another part of the exciting, pleasant world he has known since he was three. Attitude towards school by the home is now known to be a major factor in the child's learning process. The five-year-old who has not been to a nursery class or playgroup enters school clothed in the attitudes of his home—which may be favourable or unfavourable to school. The ex-nursery entrant comes with his attitude coloured by his experience of the past two years, and this alone in many cases should give him a head start, particularly as he will know that school is a place where he will be able to do the things that are asked of him. We do not sufficiently appreciate the sheer terror in the heart of a five-year-old entering the Infant School, who often imagines that he will have to do the unbelievably difficult things his older brothers and sisters have to do at school. To know that he can do the things that are done in school is a great comfort.

Finally, there is the important matter of emotional development and control. Even in the most relaxed nursery the child lives in a context of order which is based upon simple rules, which will be few in number and unobtrusive. He cannot do exactly as he wishes all the time. Inevitably there come moments when he must give way to others, wait his turn, clear something up, go out when he is told, hang his coat on his own hook—not somebody else's, etc. And this is not easy at three. He has strong emotions which may surface in short, sharp and uncontrollable outbursts. At first he will not really play *with* his class-mates, but in parallel with them, but gradually he will learn to control his emotions, to endure the disappointment of having to defer to others quite philosophically. He will become a social being.

In the small circle of the home, for most hours of the day consisting only of his mother and himself, he does not learn how to live with others nearly as effectively as in a group of his peers.

To summarize, nursery education is about play—nature's teacher; it is about language without which intellectual growth is impeded; it is about confidence and attitude to school; finally, it is about emotional development and learning to live happily with others. For all these reasons there is an overwhelming case for nursery education for the vast majority of our children, not to replace the home but to supplement it. The following chapter outlines the long struggle to achieve this. Chapter 7 sets out a plan to achieve it in the present decade.

6. The Struggle

The present provision for the pre-school child, or, more accurately, the lack of it, can only be understood by looking at the way in which our schools developed in the 19th century. Throughout most of the century there were more three-year-olds in school than there are today, though large numbers of children received no schooling of any kind until the last quarter of the century. Many of those who attended did so for a very short period, sometimes one or two years and often only for half time, after acquiring the barest minimum of instruction in the 3 Rs.

There is no separate history of nursery schools—indeed the term was not used with any degree of definition until 1908. The story of the education of the very young child, the pre-school child in today's terminology, is to be found in the growth of popular education under the pressures of industrialism, philanthropy and denominational rivalry.

In the last quarter of the 18th century the new factories, mills and mines were demanding more and more labour. At the same time mechanical production was putting the cottage craftsman out of business. Larger and larger numbers of people from the rural areas began to make their way into the new industrial towns to find work. Young children no less than their parents were forced into the apparently insatiable maw of the industrial system. The social upheaval was such that at the turn of the century those who were receiving even the rudiments of literacy were probably fewer than three hundred years previously.

However, the spectacle of vast and increasing numbers of children from the age of three upwards working incredibly long hours in appalling conditions aroused the humanitarianism which was one of the redeeming features of the early 19th century. Human concern for their plight, allied with the missionary zeal of the Churches, was often expressed in a demand for the education of the poor. The Sunday

Schools were first in the field of popular education before the end of the 18th century. In 1780 Robert Raikes established a "dame Sunday School for ragged and turbulent boys." The Sunday schools which followed made little provision for children under the age of six. They taught mainly the 3 Rs and gave religious instruction. By the early 1800s they had 850,000 children attending them from the age of three. At the same time there were about 50,000 children at Dame Schools. They were almost entirely concerned with child-minding—"the nurse collected the children of many families into her own house."[33] The dames live on today in large numbers but are now known as child-minders.

Considerable impetus was given to mass instruction by the invention of the monitorial system. Both Andrew Bell and Joseph Lancaster claimed to be its parent, although it was in use in Paris a century before either of them. In it the master instructed a number of monitors and they in turn instructed the younger children. Later in the century it evolved into the Pupil-Teacher system. In the early 1970s the educational merits of a system in which one child instructs another are again attracting attention. The work of Ronald and Peggy Pippett in the University of Michigan has led to the introduction of tutoring on a large scale in American schools and to a number of similar projects in Britain.

Both the Non-Conformist and Anglican Churches were active in establishing schools, the former through the British and Foreign School Society and the Church of England through the National Society for Promoting the Education of the Poor in the Principles of the Established Church. These two societies provided most of the schools throughout the 19th century—even after the passing of the Education Act of 1870. Their rivalry was at once one of the major impediments to the development of a national system of education and, at the same time, a spur to the establishment of schools. Although at first their schools catered for the six- to ten-year-olds they quickly lowered the starting age to three. This change was accelerated by the passing of the Factory Act of 1833, which banned the employment of children under nine in the textile industry and limited the working week to a maximum of forty-eight hours up to the age of thirteen. In the same year the first grant of public money was given for the "education of children of the poorer classes." £20,000 was made available to the two Societies—a method of financing school development which was used throughout most of the century. The annual grant had reached £800,000 by 1870. By this time there was also a fairly large amount of money being devoted to education from other sources. This including royal begging letters, educational charities and, on occasions, even free postage. In 1870 there were about two million children in school, although some were there for very short periods, and a great many as half-timers.

This growth in numbers had been possible because the provisions of the Factory Act of 1833 had by now been applied to other industries, and young children who were in the main barred from employment were free to attend school.

In the meantime the problem of asserting central financial control over a nation-wide but very diverse system of schools provided by voluntary bodies but which were largely publicly financed had been solved in a way by Robert Lowe's Revised Code of 1862. This laid down a minimum syllabus in the 3 Rs and introduced payment by results. By doing so it virtually demolished the monitorial system at a stroke. Mass instruction was no longer appropriate. Each child had to be taught as an individual and the teacher's salary depended on the result. Although the grants were paid on each child from six to twelve who passed the inspectors' tests, they could also apply to the three- to six-year-olds at the discretion of the inspector.

The Revised Code forced a rapid and radical change in teaching methods. It was a crash literacy programme and, as such, if for no other reason, could be justified as making the content of elementary education relevant to the needs of mid-Victorian society. Nevertheless the system was rigid and narrow. In place of a commendably broad curriculum which had been developing in the schools it led to over-emphasis, indeed brutal over-emphasis, on mechanical competence in the 3 Rs. For the next forty years it prevented any evolution of teaching methods for the majority of young children.

This was particularly unfortunate because side by side with the schools provided by the two societies there were also progressive, independent infant schools established by private individuals, and influenced in their methods by the ideas on the education of young children which were being developed on the Continent. They were based on ". . . a richer and fuller educational tradition than that of the contemporary monitorial day schools."[34] There were a number of successful experimental infant schools in Europe. The earliest was established at Waldbach, Alsace, in 1769 by J. F. Oberein (1740–1826), the pastor of the parish. There is some doubt about who should have the

credit for the first British infant school. It was established at New
Lanark by Robert Owen in 1816 and he claimed, and is usually given,
the credit for the remarkably enlightened methods developed there. But
the late Professor Robert R. Rusk held the view that it owed very much
more to a gifted teacher named James Buchanan, who was employed
there than to Owen himself. The probable explanation is that Owen, at
first at any rate, was mainly concerned with having the children looked
after in safety to allow their mothers to work in his mill, and that it was
Buchanan with his flute and his genius for communicating with young
children who developed the techniques which were to acquire an inter-
national reputation for the school.

Buchanan left New Lanark in 1819 and established an infant school
at Vincent Square, Westminster—the first in England. His methods
were copied by Samuel Wilderspin, a vain but able man, who eventually
founded his own school and, as Owen had done earlier, claimed to be
the originator of the infant school—a claim which Lord Brougham con-
tested vigorously in his defence of Buchanan. Nevertheless Wilderspin
propagated the formation of infant schools with great missionary zeal.
Eventually the Home and Colonial Infant School Society was formed to
foster the establishment of infant schools and to train teachers for them.
It owed a great deal of its inspiration to Dr Charles Mayo and Elizabeth
Mayo. Very soon there were some hundreds of schools and the two
denominational societies began to provide infant departments as part of
their own schools. The existence of large numbers of schools catering
for the five- to eight-year-old group probably induced Mr Forster to
choose a starting age of five, which was much lower than in other countries—or maybe it was because Aristotle in his *Politics* made from birth
to five one of his stages of infancy. Although today we are unfortunately
short of places for our pre-school children we do at least have a very low
compulsory starting age, and for this we can thank the independent infant school movement of the 19th century.

Throughout the century the methods used in these schools were
refreshingly progressive and, of course, being independent, they did not
suffer the effects of the revised code imposed on the schools of the two
societies and, later, the board schools. Their main inspiration came
from the work of Jean Pestalozzi (1746–1827) in Switzerland, and
Friedrich Froebel (1782–1852) in Germany. Owen visited Pestalozzi's
school at Yverdun and Mayo actually spent some years there. Mayo
was so enthusiastic at the methods he saw there that he established a

Pestalozzian School on his return to England in 1821 and he taught in it for the rest of his life.

There is something of a parallel between Pestalozzi and Truby King. Each became interested in the upbringing of children by first taking into his own home a number of orphans and both were deeply interested in practical farming. From Pestalozzi's experience with these children and his observation of his own son's growth he was able to develop his ideas on education which he recorded in *How Father Pestalozzi Educated and Observed his three-and-a-half-year-old Son*, his *Addresses* and many other works. He established his school at Yverdun to put his theories into practice. It was concerned with the whole child—physical, moral, emotional and intellectual. It had a rich and varied curriculum and insisted on preserving the closest contact with the homes of its children—indeed a number of Pestalozzi's works consist of detailed advice to mothers in teaching their children to observe and talk. His methods were based upon the development of language, number and form. The handling of objects was a central feature in them. They were very important in arithmetic but were used in drawing to inculcate an appreciation of form. In *The ABC of Observation* he set out a detailed scheme for observing and naming "differences in form and relation between several objects." Elizabeth Mayo in her book *Lessons on Objects* . . . was influenced by what she had seen at Yverdun, though she clearly had not really understood it. Her insistence on pointing out the actual qualities of objects which she borrowed from Pestalozzi gave birth to the Object Lesson which held sway in English education until well into the 20th century. Miss Mayo was not alone among English observers and imitators of Pestalozzi who rather missed the point. Others fell short of his philosophy and methods when they tried to import them into the new infant schools. It was not until the German Kindergarten movement was started by Froebel, who had been greatly influenced by the school at Yverdun, as well as by Rousseau, that Pestalozzi's influence on English schools revived. Oddly enough Froebel did not make his major impact in England until his books were translated after his death, between 1885 and 1893. The two men were very different. Pestalozzi was essentially an empiricist but Froebel brought a trained, philosophic mind to bear on education. Although they were different they were complementary to each other. Pestalozzi's influence would have run into the sand without the skilful advocacy of Froebel.

The popularizing of his ideas in this country owed much to the Baroness von Marenholtz-Bülow, to the Society of Arts who exhibited Froebel apparatus in 1854, and to Charles Dickens who advocated "Infant Gardens" and very wisely warned against the danger of the system becoming too formal. The Froebel Society was formed in 1874, largely by Emily Shirreff and Maria Grey. Its purpose was to disseminate Froebel's methods and to train teachers in them. Froebel saw play as the central activity of the young, and as having great educational value. An appropriate learning environment would, through the use of carefully devised apparatus, and a broad curriculum, direct play so that his children grew both intellectually and physically. He believed in and encouraged make-believe—often gratuitously and where it was not needed. It was mainly because of his attitude to make-believe that the followers of Dr Montessori parted company from the original Froebel theory in the early years of the present century.

Froebel gave infant education a coherent scheme of teaching founded for the first time upon the nature of young children but always related to and supplementary to the educational influence of the home.

The Education Act of 1870 was intended to fill the gaps in the education system. School Boards were created to establish schools where they were needed. The boards had the power to make attendance compulsory between the ages of five and thirteen, with exemptions, if they wished to do so. The passing of this Act spurred the two voluntary societies to a new lease of life because of the competition from the new secular school boards. During the next seven years they provided over one million additional places compared with fewer than two million in the thirty-one years preceding 1870. Ten years later a further Education Act turned the power to enforce compulsory attendance, into a duty.

The board schools usually had infant departments, often under their own mistresses. Three-year-olds were almost always admitted and continued to be eligible for grant. It has been estimated that at the time of the Forster Act about a quarter of this age-group attended school. Payment by results remained until 1897, but before the system was abolished, and indeed after the 1870 Act Froebel methods were coming into wider use. A large free kindergarten was established in Salford in 1873 by Sir William Mather. This provided meals and baths for the children and had a teacher from a Berlin Kindergarten. In 1874 the London School Board appointed a lecturer on Froebel methods and the British Society established a kindergarten college and practising school at Stockwell. Nevertheless the Cross Commission of 1886, an inquiry into the whole field of elementary education, made no mention of the Kindergarten movement. However, between 1870 and 1900 the number of three- to five-year-olds attending school had increased from 24 per cent to 43 per cent of these age-groups. The highest point reached was in the first year of the present century when it was almost three times the percentage in 1972. It looked as though the English education system was set permanently to provide for the child below the statutory starting age in the board schools as well as the independent infant schools and kindergartens.

However, this was not to be. Shortly after local education authorities were established in 1902 they were allowed to refuse admission to the under-fives. As a result the number of pre-school children attending started to decline rapidly, and has never again approached the peak of the turn of the century. Between 1900 and 1910 it fell to about 23 per cent and to about 15 per cent by 1920. In 1930 it was 13 per cent and in 1972 it is 11·5 per cent. As the cost of the growing education system increased the pre-school child was seen as a low priority. This quite deliberate policy after 1902 of not providing for more than a small proportion of the three-to-five age-group created the pre-school problem which, seventy years later, is still very far from being resolved. But their virtual exclusion from school gave both an identity and a stimulus to the nursery schools, which were making by far the most valuable and distinctive contribution to English education, as the Primary Schools and pre-school playgroups are doing in the 1970s.

The long line of inspired teachers of young children—Pestalozzi, Buchanan, Wilderspin, Froebel, Montessori—was continued in the early years of this century with the most successful of all, Margaret McMillan (1860–1931) and her sister Rachel (1859–1917). In 1914, after years of campaigning on the importance of health in the education of young children, they started their open-air nursery school at Deptford. In a century and a half of imaginative experiment in the independent infant schools, this school probably had a greater influence than any other single school on the subsequent development of nursery education.

The children were dispersed in six low shelters around a central garden to reduce the danger of infection, and a great deal of activity took place out of doors. Each shelter had thirty-five to fifty children and was equipped with its own cloakrooms, bathrooms and toilets. The garden was laid out as an attractive play area with aviary, pet-corners, jungle gym, slide, etc. It was staffed by qualified teachers, assisted by students from the adjoining nursery-school training college. The school was open from 7.30 a.m. until 5.30 in the afternoon. Breakfast, dinner and tea was available for those who wanted it. The methods were based on free activity, handwork, music and games. The open-air pattern became a model for nursery schools until medical control of infection became more effective after the second world war and dispersal was no longer necessary.

A particularly valuable feature was the mothers' club, which met once a week—a degree of parental involvement in nursery education which we have been in danger of losing until the remarkable growth of the playgroup movement in recent years. Indeed many playgroups today are preceded by mothers' clubs.

There were other pioneering schools in Notting Hill, Manchester and Sheffield. Detailed descriptions of all four are given in Appendix IV of the Hadow Report of 1933.[34]

Throughout this period Dr Maria Montessori had a considerable influence on the education of young children in Britain. Her methods borrowed a good deal from Edouard Sequin (1812–88). He was concerned with handicapped children and developed apparatus for sensory training and for the development of concepts of form and number. Dr Montessori created similar apparatus for normal children. The major criticisms of her system were first, that it was a system and like most systems became somewhat rigid. Secondly, she insisted on an over-prepared environment generally in school as well as in the over-systematized provision of apparatus. This inhibited free activity and free imagination. Her apparatus tended to become teacher-directed, but in the McMillan school the teacher's posture was one of skilled non-intervention. Nevertheless a great deal of the present preoccupation of nursery and infant teachers with the assembling of resources for learning is traceable to her method. In this she made a major contribution to the richness and vitality of our nursery schools.

The Consultative Committee Report published in 1908 after an inquiry into the "... desirability, or otherwise, both on educational and on other grounds, of discouraging the attendance at school of children under five years" said that "... nursery schools are in a great many cases a practical necessity." It went on to say that the option of attending should be given at three.[35] In spite of this weighty support the numbers of children attending them continued to drop rapidly and no attempt was made to implement the report until the Education Act of 1918. Local Education Authorities were then given the power to supply or aid nursery schools or nursery classes for children over two and under five years of age but only for those ". . . whose attendance at such a school is necessary or desirable for their healthy, physical and mental development."

There was little immediate growth in the nursery school movement until the 1930s, when it developed rather more rapidly. By 1939 114 nursery schools had been opened by 58 local education authorities and 56 by other organizations catering for about 10,000 children. A great many of these became residential nurseries during the war and by 1945 there were over 400 of them. In the meantime local maternity and child-welfare authorities opened about 1400 day nurseries for the pre-school children of women engaged on war work.

When Parliament came to replace the 1918 Act in 1944 it appeared to have legislated for the universal provision of nursery education. Local education authorities in fulfilling their duty to provide sufficient schools in their areas had to have regard, *inter alia,* to the "need for securing that provision is made for pupils who have not attained the age of five years by the provision of nursery schools or . . . of nursery classes. . . ." (Section 8.)

They were also to submit development plans to the Minister and among the requirements they were asked to "give particulars of the arrangements made and proposed to be made by the Authority for meeting the needs of pupils who have not attained the age of five . . . ." (Section 11.) Unfortunately there was a catch in it! The *duty* to which this refers was to be measured by the criterion of "providing primary education, that is to say, full-time education, suitable to the requirements of junior pupils." (Section 8.) And "compulsory school age" is later defined as any age between five and fifteen years. Thus there was no breach of duty by a local education authority which took no steps to implement the part of their development plan which referred to nursery schools.

The diffuseness of the 1944 Act's reference to nursery education and the very high post-war birth-rate which increased the size, and the cost, of the problem together with the vast cost of providing meaningful secondary education effectively prevented any significant post-war development. Indeed, the low priority given to pre-school education was recognized by the Government in 1960 by the issue of Circular 8/60 which forbade the provision of any additional nursery schools or classes although it asked local education authorities not to reduce their existing number of places and also to consider using them on a half-time basis where this was not already being done, so that more children could benefit from them. This circular had not the force of law but until the early '70s local education authorities were prepared to accept it as a prohibition of nursery school expansion.

It was cancelled by the Government's White Paper in December 1972.[36] Up to that time local authorities regarded it as prohibiting nursery school expansion, but there were two further developments. The first, made in 1964 and 1965, allowed new places to be provided to accommodate the children of women teachers returning to teaching. This change has produced about four thousand full-time equivalent places, not all, or even a majority, of which are now used by the children of teachers. Indeed it is now quite common to find whole classes formed under these circulars without any teachers' children. The second and much more important change was made by the Urban Aid Programme started by the Labour Government in 1968, and continued by the subsequent Conservative administration. This had provided 17,790 full-time equivalent places up to the summer of 1972.

This major modification of the policy of Circular 8/60 was inspired by the Plowden Report (1966), which examined a good deal of evidence on the influence of environment on a child's chances of fulfilling his educational potential.[16] The report played a major part in focusing the attention of the world of education on the connection between deprivation and education and on the importance of the early years if compensatory education is to be effective. In addition, it found a considerable consensus on the value of nursery education among 1,852 primary school teachers questioned—73 per cent thought it should be available to *all* children whose parents wanted it. Twenty-two per cent thought it should only be available for children in special need of help and only 2·7 per cent were opposed to any provision.

The report's unequivocal support for nursery education and the detailed plans it suggested for expansion have given an impetus to the vigorous campaign by such bodies as the National Campaign for Nursery Education, the Pre-School Playgroups Association, the Save the Children Fund, the Nursery School Association, the National Society of Children's Nurseries, etc. They regard the Urban Aid

Programme as a partial success for their campaign and this has whetted their appetite all the more. By 1972 when a petition with 365,000 signatures was presented to Parliament they had become the most active and articulate pressure group in a service which abounds with them.

The percentages of the pre-school age-groups in full-time attendance at school in England and Wales in January 1971 and the number of children were as follows:

2 years	$0.2 =$	1,411
3 years	$2.3 =$	18,294
4 years	$31.5 =$	258,840
2–4 years	$11.5 =$	278,545
3–4 years	$16.3 =$	277,134

This includes maintained, direct grant and independent schools of all types.

In addition there were 22,574 attending day nurseries in 1972 and an estimated two hundred thousand in playgroups. Thus out of a total three-four age group of 1,631,000, about a third receive pre-school education of some kind—if day nurseries are included and child-minding is omitted.

There are large numbers of children in the daily care of child-minders, some good but many illegal and unregistered, and often using sordid and indeed dangerous premises; e.g. in the Paddington area, of seventeen illegal minders three lived in one room and each looked after nine or ten children. In December 1970 there were 83,000 children in the care of registered child-minders but there is no information about the large numbers looked after by unregistered minders. Attention was recently focused on this problem by Sonia Jackson in a detailed review.[37]

Thus, in spite of a century of often exciting history, many sympathetic official reports, two superficially helpful Acts of Parliament, a stream of convincing research findings, an increasingly enthusiastic public opinion, the picture is far from satisfactory. It is patchy in the extreme both in the extent of the provision and in the quality of it.

Although it is difficult to make comparisons because of the low statutory starting age in Britain, other western countries take the pre-school child more seriously than we do in deciding their educational priorities.

In Italy, a country with acute educational problems, a law introducing state nursery schools was passed in 1968. Today more than half the three- to five-year-olds attend school—a proportion which is far in excess of ours. A major aim of the law is to give poorer children a chance of starting the primary school with similar attainments to those of the middle-class child.

The French compulsory schooling age is six, but virtually all children in France of five are in school and 63 per cent of the two-to-six age-group attend nursery school. As ambitious building programme is being undertaken with the aim of providing for 90 per cent of four-year-olds and 62 per cent of three-year-olds by 1976. At present class sizes are large by British standards. The average nursery school class has forty-five children on the roll, but the average attendance is between thirty-five and forty. The teaching is extremely rigid; e.g. the Government lays it down that each five-year-old must spend ten hours each week in the study of French.

A movement rather similar to the Pre-School Playgroup Movement in Britain has led to the growth of small, independent nursery groups in France, especially on Thursdays when the schools are closed. In addition there are many private nursery schools charging quite high fees.

Germany also has a statutory starting age of six, but there were in 1969 places for about 37 per cent of the three-to-five age-group. Approximately half of the five-year age-group attend school, compared with 100 per cent in France. The aim is to lower the compulsory starting age to five years by 1980 and by the same date to make nursery places available for 75 per cent of children above the age of three. A great many of the kindergartens are privately provided, frequently by the churches, although the fees are lower than those of the private nursery schools in France. An increasing, though still small, part of pre-school education is now being provided in vorklassen (nursery classes) attached to the primary schools. There are four hundred of these classes in West Berlin alone.

The western country which has come nearest to providing nursery education for all who want it for their children is Belgium. About 95 per cent of pre-school children from three years upwards attend the schools which are free. Almost always the nursery school is part of the primary school. Belgium's good record in the extent of pre-school provision is partly a product of the religious division in the country and the desire to achieve parity of treatment for the two communities. There are signs however that the nursery schools are tending to develop into something approaching our day nurseries in which children are left for up to twelve hours a day.

The United States has looked to the nursery school perhaps more than any other western country as a means of helping disadvantaged children to take their place in school on equal terms with the rest. In the 1930s Federal Government aid was given through the Works Progress Administration to counter the deprivations suffered by children and teachers in the economic depression. During the Second World War aid was given to nursery schools on a fairly wide scale through the Lanham Act to enable mothers to undertake war work. As in Britain, with our war-time day nurseries, most of the schools were closed at the end of the war though some were taken over by the local communities.

In 1964 the Economic Opportunity Act again enabled Federal aid to be given. The following year Head Start summer schools appeared and eventually extended to the full year. Their aim was to make good the cultural and social disadvantage suffered by many children so that they could take full advantage of their statutory schooling. In 1969 the Federal Government set up the Office of Child Development under the Secretary of the Department of Health, Education and Welfare. The Office was required to take a comprehensive approach to the physical, social and intellectual development of young children.

Head Start had a budget of £40m. in 1965; today it is £160m. It is of course much more than pre-school education. It involves a whole complex of related services and has always encouraged parental co-operation on a commendable scale. Unfortunately it only reaches one in five of those eligible for it.

These five examples illustrate the importance attached to the pre-school years in the education systems of other countries. Italy, France and Germany are ahead of Britain, yet all have ambitious plans for expansion. Belgium has already provided as many places as are ever likely to be required. The United States is taking an active and intelligent interest in the needs of the young child. The time has now come for Britain to make its plans and find the resources to enable them to be carried out. And the mid-'70s are the most propitious period to do so for many years.

7. Plan for Expansion

As the educational and social benefits of pre-school education have become more widely understood and accepted the pressure for places has increased enormously. It comes partly from parents who, in addition to their growing interest in the education of their children, often need the second income which a nursery place for a pre-school child makes possible. Probably half a million mothers with pre-school children go out to work. The Plowden Report suggested that the economic benefit from the additional employment of married women which would result from an expansion of nursery education would cover about one third of the cost.[16] This is one of the few areas where at least part of the economic return from additional expenditure on education is reasonably easy to assess. But there is also an extremely strong professional demand from both teachers' unions and such local authority organizations as the Association of Education Committees.

The pressure has been increased by the provision of an additional 17,000 places between 1969 and 1972 under the Urban Aid Programme, by the growth of the playgroup movement and by the growing reluctance of local education authorities to accept the restriction imposed by Circular 8/60, which, they now realize, was a voluntary and not a legal restriction. As places have been provided the demand for them has grown. The primary school headmistress with a nursery class attached almost lives in a state of permanent siege from parents whose children cannot be accepted.

There is now virtually a universal acceptance that a diversion of resources into the pre-school sector of the education system is a first priority for the present decade. But in addition to this it is an appropriate time for expansion for two other reasons. First, in the second half of the '60s the number of teachers in training increased by 86 per cent, and, consequently, the teaching force is improving more rapidly than ever before. Approximately 18,000–20,000 additional teachers are now available each year. Professional, as well as lay opinion will rightly demand that most of these should be used to reduce the size of classes. But as the decade goes on more and more of them can be made available for nursery teaching—provided training courses are organized in the colleges of education in time and in sufficient numbers.

Secondly, the time for expansion is appropriate for demographic reasons. The number of children in primary schools will fall by about a quarter of a million by the end of the '70s. Some of these vacant places are in slum schools due for early replacement in the older industrial cities and will cease to exist. Others will be needed to reduce the size of classes, for class size is the product of two factors—teachers and school places. But after allowing for places which cease to exist in obsolescent schools and those which are used to lower the size of classes, there will remain a considerable and growing increment of places each year in the decade which could be used by pre-school children; for example, in 1973 the primary school population will fall by 35,000. It is reasonable to assume that of these 10,000 places could be made available for the under-fives. By the end of the '70s there will probably be 70,000, which could be used without erecting additional class-rooms, though of course some modification would be needed.

Thus, for the first time, there is the public and professional will to expand, an adequate teacher supply and a bonus of space in primary schools which will greatly reduce the capital cost of a programme of expansion.

The size of the demand is impossible to estimate with accuracy if pre-school education is to remain voluntary, as it surely must.

The Plowden Council (1967) estimated that places should be provided for 50 per cent of three-year-olds and 90 per cent of four-year-olds, and that, of these, 15 per cent should be full-time places and the rest half-time.[16] This estimate is accepted in the 1972 White Paper.[36] But there can be little doubt that these assumptions about take-up are now too low. Nevertheless it is extremely difficult to quantify the growing demand. Tessa Blackstone has placed it at 75 per cent for three-year-olds, and based her cost estimates on this figure.[38] Six experienced Chief Education Officers consulted felt that the Plowden figure for both the three-year-old group and for full-time places were too low, but most were unwilling to hazard a guess at what they should now be.

In spite of the difficulty it is important to make the most intelligent guess possible, and guess it must be, and base a programme of expansion upon it. If, in the event, it proves to be either an underestimate or an overestimate the programme can be adjusted. There is general agreement that demand is considerable, and it is the worst possible excuse for delaying a plan to meet it that it cannot be exactly measured. The 75 per cent figure used by Tessa Blackstone has been adopted in the plan set out below rather than the Plowden and White Paper figure of 50 per cent.[36]

The number of full-time places to be provided depends initially of course upon the decision as to whether or not the general objective should be to provide full-time or part-time pre-school education. Professional opinion—and probably parental opinion also—now appears on balance to be more favourable to half-day attendance. The number of half-time nursery places has increased from 4,000 to 58,000 in the past eleven years. An exception to this view is the mother who from sheer economic necessity cannot wait to get her child into school full-time so that she can go out to work.

A whole school-day is much too long for the three- or four-year-old to be away from his mother and the security she gives him, particularly at meal times or sleeping times. And the noise and bustle of the modern nursery class are a considerable strain on him.

If we compare the quiet life of most children at home up to the age of three, particularly if they are only children, with the maelstrom of the nursery, and try to look at it from their point of view and not from that of an adult, we may begin to appreciate what an upsetting experience it can be at first.

Half-day attendance is by far the most effective for the under-fives. Full-time may actually be counter-productive by causing frustration, aggressive and even violent behaviour. It is worth remembering that we have the lowest starting age for compulsory education in Western Europe. The case for restricting attendance to half a day under five is overwhelming, but there is also an economic consideration. If pre-school education is to be available for all who want it for their children by the end of the present decade, it will siphon off fewer resources from the rest of the education system if it is provided in this way rather than on a completely full-time basis. To put it bluntly it will be cheaper and, consequently, it is more likely to be carried through.

But the general pattern of half-time attendance must, as Plowden recognized, be modified in the case of a sizeable minority of children who will need to attend full-time from the start. In view of all we now know of the effects of deprivation on performance at school (see Chapter 4), the Plowden estimate of 15 per cent will almost certainly be too low and its acceptance is a major defect in the government's plan for expansion. Probably 20 per cent would be nearer the mark, though that also may well prove to be too low.

Some of the factors which give rise to the category of children who need to be in school full-time have increased since 1967: for example, the divorce and illegitimacy rates.

Sir Alec Clegg and Barbara Megson have set out a number of conditions which create special problems for children.[39] They are:

> Poverty
> Squalor
> Cruelty
> Sick or dying parent
> Immorality
> Deranged mother
> Children in care of wrong parent
> The family drudge
> Parent who has given up
> Quarrelling
> Illegitimate child

They call the children who suffer from these conditions "children in distress," i.e. "children who are wretchedly unhappy because of the strain put upon them at home." They estimated that in the West Riding of Yorkshire 25,000 to 30,000 children needed preventive help, but received little of it, in addition to the 5,000 who were receiving curative help. If these figures are an indication of the number of children in distress nationally they are a significant minority who require special educational attention including, in almost all cases, full-time pre-school provision.

There are, of course, other groups for whom full-time attendance would be desirable; for example, the child of the widowed mother who must take a job in order to maintain herself and her child, and the illegitimate child.

The figures below are based on the following assumptions about demand:

Age-group	Number of Places required
3-year	75 per cent of age-group
4-year	90 per cent of age-group

80 per cent of the places for each age group provided to be half-time and 20 per cent full-time.

Having decided the objective in terms of places the second major decision needed is the time it is proposed to take to reach the above standards of provision—over how many years should the expansion programme be spread? The government's plan is presumably spread over about ten years.

The Registrar-General estimates that the size of the age-groups at the beginning of the 1980s will be:

3 years	817,000	(75% = 612,000)
4 years	819,000	(90% = 737,000)

On present trends it is reasonable to assume that the two groups will re-main around these figures throughout the 1980s, or slightly less. Thus to meet the probable demand in the 1980s we need to plan now to make the following places available.

20 per cent of 1,349,000 =   269,000 (full-time)
80 per cent of 1,349,000 = 1,079,000 (half-time)

Total full-time equivalent places $= \dfrac{1,079,000}{2} + 269,000 = 810,000$

(rounded). The White Paper objective is for 700,000 places by 1981 because it is based on the lower Plowden estimates of demand.[36]

The number of pre-school children in maintained schools in January 1971 was 261,000 including four-year-olds and rising-fives, i.e. children admitted to school in the term before their fifth birthday, in primary schools. If present trends in pre-school attendance continue, and it is reasonable to assume that they will do so, ten years hence (1982) this figure will have increased to approximately 420,000. The White Paper estimate is 450,000.

The above objective calls for a total of 810,000 places by the end of the decade. Without an expansion programme there will be 420,000. It follows that the programme must plan to create 390,000 (rounded to 400,000) additional places.

The above figures of present and projected provision have left out of account the three-to-four-year-olds in direct grant or independent schools. The numbers are extremely small, amounting to 0·3 per cent of three-year-olds and 1·7 per cent of four-year-olds compared with 1·9 per cent and 29·8 per cent respectively in maintained schools (January 1971).

Equally, the 200,000 children attending registered Pre-School Playgroups have not been included in the total of existing places. They are a much more significant group, both numerically, amounting to 8·1 per cent of the two age-groups, and educationally. Grants are made by the Department of Health and Social Security and by the Department of Education and Science to the Pre-School Playgroups Association, to help to finance their headquarters and the employment of organizers. Local Authorities in many cases also give financial and other assistance to the groups, though the amount of help given varies considerably from one area to another. (See Chapter 9.) Any pre-school expansion plan must contain an assumption about the part, if any, the voluntary groups will play. Are they to be regarded as stop-gap provision of pre-school education until nursery places are universally available and consequently ignored in assessing the number of places to be provided, or are they to be regarded as a valuable example of community self-help to be retained, given assistance and taken into account in the final provision of places?

Because of the numbers already involved, and they are increasing quite quickly, the answer has an important bearing on the logistics of pre-school provision. First, it is important to dispel any fear that the voluntary playgroup movement is in any way analogous to the independent secondary and primary schools, which are privately owned, often as lucrative businesses, by individual or corporate bodies. In the main independent schools exist to preserve class privilege. The playgroups on the other hand are organized and run by parents in rented premises in their own communities and frequently receive local authority assistance. Their two great merits are, first that they involve parents in the education of their children in a way and to an extent which could well be copied in the maintained nursery and primary schools. Second, they are as much concerned with the education of mothers as they are with their children. In this they have brought a new and very welcome change of view about pre-school education. Whatever provision we make, the mother is the young child's principal teacher. She is almost always untrained and ill-equipped for such tasks as teaching her child his native language, the selection of appropriate play material, etc. The nursery teacher and, usually, the playgroup leader are able to help her and, because of this, there are the strongest arguments for involving parents on a regular, organized basis in nursery schools and classes. In its degree of parental involvement the voluntary playgroup movement has made a major contribution to the education of young children which may well more than compensate for the rather meagre professional training of its leaders.

The playgroup is not run by outsiders coming to the area each day in their cars, but by the local community itself, by Mrs Smith next door and Mrs Jones in the next street, and all the parents have their rota turn to help.

It is the community looking after its own children, equipping them to live in that community. The three-year-old entering it is not thrown into an alien culture of unfamiliar faces, accents, values, but into a warm, friendly extension of his own community. In a slum area of Newcastle, where the houses are deteriorating rapidly and a large Asian immigrant population is concentrated, the local Tenants' Association runs its own group in a house which will eventually be demolished. Seeing it, one cannot escape the feeling that, given some outside help, its vitality and warmth would be well worth the sacrifice of some of the clinical atmosphere and profusion of commercially produced equipment which are to be found in the maintained nursery schools provided under the Urban Programme. It is an example of a community which society has neglected and allowed to become down at heel and demoralized, pulling itself up by its own stocking-tops. And, human nature being what it is, the chances of success are much higher than if their "betters" tried to do it for them. Of course they need help, physical help and advice, but sensitively given and only when they feel the need for it.

In the past it has been a valid criticism of the movement that it operated mainly in lush middle-class areas, but this is now much less true; for example, the London Borough of Southwark has forty-eight registered playgroups of which fourteen are organized by the Save the Children Fund, twenty by the Pre-School Playgroups Association and fourteen by independent persons. Many are in working-class areas. Indeed the whole borough has been defined as a socially deprived area.[40] Anyhow the prosperous suburb is also a community often as much in need of help, though of a different kind, as the down-town area, and community self-help is just as welcome there.

It would be sheer lunacy to dissipate the benefits which have flowed from this national, grass-roots initiative in recent years. Its rapid growth has been a remarkable educational phenomenon which no one except the incorrigible bureaucrat or the rigid stickler for professionalism would wish to destroy. Its vitality is influencing for the good pre-school education generally in rather the same way as the Open University is acting like leaven throughout the whole field of higher education. Its social benefits, particularly to families in deprived areas, are as important as its educational benefits. Even if it were desirable to do so, it is extremely doubtful whether it could be destroyed with anything short of the most draconian legislation.

For all these reasons, it is assumed that the voluntary playgroup movement will have a permanent place in our pattern of pre-school provision of about its present size. The 200,000 children in the groups attend part-time in the main. Usually "part-time" is less than half-time and for this reason it is difficult to express present playgroup provision in full-time place equivalents. On the assumption that three half-days a week is about the average, it probably amounts to 60,000 full-time equivalent places, and provision is made for this number. But if they are to be included they will need assistance to improve some of their less satisfactory features. This would be partly capital assistance to help in the purchase of equipment. It would also involve help towards recurrent expenditure in educational priority areas; for example, the financing of an adequate fee-remission scheme, the training of leaders, and an advisory service.

The expenditure figures below include capital grants to all recognized groups, but £50 p.a. grants per full-time equivalent place towards running costs only to groups in educational priority areas.

In return for financial and advisory assistance groups would be required to register with the local education authority. This would replace the present registration requirements and would be part of the responsibility of the education department of the local authority, not the social services department as at present and as recommended by a majority of the Seebohm inquiry.[41] They would be open to inspection on both health and educational grounds. A number of registered groups would be affiliated to a nursery school or primary school with nursery class. Each of these groupings of maintained provision with affiliated voluntary groups would have its own pre-school committee of teachers, group-leaders and parents. A special post could be created under the Burnham Scales for a teacher in the nursery school or nursery class who would be responsible for liaison with the playgroups and advice to them. Local education authorities would also be expected to appoint Playgroup Organizers as some do now. Plowden[16] suggested nursery centres and Halsey[31] has carried the idea forward with a proposal for hybrid centres consisting of playgroups grouped around LEA nursery schools, classes or primary schools. Day nurseries would also be included. This is a statutory-voluntary partnership.

In addition to these loose arrangements for bringing the playgroups into regular contact with the schools it would probably be beneficial to develop a national qualification for leaders, although there are obvious dangers in doing so.

In addition it would be of benefit to both the teaching profession and the playgroups if the liaison proposed in the nursery centres could be started in the training of leaders by encouraging colleges of education to undertake this work, as some do now, wherever possible.

Playgroup leaders must have the stimulus and advice which only the professional teachers can give but the groups would lose much of their attractiveness if they were over-professionalized.

It would also help to give coherence to the playgroup movement if all the national sponsoring bodies could come together to form one national organization. This should not be too difficult to achieve.

The White Paper[36] also proposes that playgroups should have a permanent place in the pattern of pre-school provision but it makes no proposals for financial assistance to them and, probably for this reason, is vague about the size of their contribution.

The number of new places for which it is necessary to plan in maintained schools now therefore is 340,000 (400,000 − 60,000). The final consideration in deciding the duration of the expansion programme is, of course, the extremely important one of capital cost. No attempt is made here to find the necessary capital resources elsewhere in the field of educational expenditure. If the nation wills pre-school education for most of its children, as it clearly does, it must be prepared to find the resources. If these are to be found from existing public expenditure rather than from increased taxation there is no logical reason why they should be sought exclusively in existing educational expenditure. There is nothing sacrosanct about the present proportion of public expenditure or of the gross domestic product devoted to education or any other service. While the cost per student in higher education could undoubtedly be reduced without impairing the quality of the education provided, the number of students in higher education will increase rapidly over the decade. Because of this it would not only be unrealistic, but positively harmful, to expand pre-school education at the expense of higher education. Both will require more resources, although the latter should be required to reduce its unit costs significantly.

The assumptions made in costing the programme about capital costs per pre-school place are, at 1971 prices:

£

(a) 520   in nursery schools

(b) 450   in nursery classes attached to primary schools where no classrooms are available

(c) 300   in nursery classes attached to primary schools where spare rooms are available which can be adapted.

(d)   50   capital grant per FTE place in pre-school playgroups in EP areas

(e)   25   capital grant per FTE place in pre-school playgroups outside EP areas

(FTE = full-time equivalent)

On these assumptions the total capital cost of the entire programme would be:

		£			£
*	(a)	520 ×	17,000	=	8,840,000
	(b)	450 ×	253,000	=	113,850,000
	(c)	300 ×	70,000	=	21,000,000
† {	(d)	50 ×	20,000	=	1,000,000
	(e)	25 ×	40,000	=	1,000,000
			400,000	plus	145,690,000

* It is assumed that 5 per cent of the new places are in nursery schools and the rest in nursery classes attached to primary schools.
† It is assumed that one-third of the places recognized and supported would be in EP areas.

Capital expenditure of this order could reasonably be undertaken in a five-year programme of authorizations which would in fact spread the expenditure over a six-year period, compared with ten years in the White Paper programme.

The only capital expenditure figures mentioned in the White Paper are £15m. for each of the years 1974–5 and 1975–6.[36]

	Year	*Authorized programme*	*Expenditure*
In EP	1	29,138,000	$\frac{1}{3}$ of authorization
Areas	2	29,138,000	whole amount
	3	29,138,000	whole amount
	4	29,138,000	whole amount
	5	29,138,000	whole amount
	6	29,138,000	$\frac{2}{3}$ of authorization

The annual recurrent costs of the programme when fully implemented have been estimated on the following assumptions, at 1971 prices:

(a) Cost per place in a nursery school £250
(b) Cost per place in a nursery class £150
(c) Annual grant for full-time equivalent place in a reorganized playgroup in an EP Area £ 50

On this basis the annual cost of the additional places will be:

(a) £250 × 17,000 = £ 4,250,000
(b) £150 × 323,000 = £48,450,000
(c) £ 50 × 20,000 = £ 1,000,000

£53,700,000

The above cost per place in nursery schools and classes make provision for a considerably lower pupil/teacher ratio than at present.

It would also be necessary to make a similar improvement in the present provision for under-fives who, it was established above, will on present trends increase to 420,000 by the early 1980s. The need to do so is urgent, particularly for the rising-fives and the four-year-olds who are being admitted by some local education authorities. At the moment in many cases this really amounts to providing nursery education on the cheap. Pre-school children admitted to a primary school ought to be in classes with a scale of provision of both teachers and nursery assistants equal to that of the nursery school.

On the rough assumption that half of the 420,000 will be in primary schools and the rest in nursery classes the cost of bringing these places up to that estimated for nursery classes (£150) would be as follows:

Present cost per primary place   = £103
∴ Additional cost = £50 × 200,000   = £10,000,000

Present cost per nursery place   = £130
∴ Additional cost = £20 × 200,000   = £4,000,000

Thus when the expansion programme is complete it will add £67·7m. (£53·7m. + £14m.) to our annual expenditure on education—equivalent to an additional 2·6 per cent on 1971 prices.

Any mention of the cost expanding pre-school education inevitably raises the issue of whether or not it should be provided free or whether fees should be charged. The Plowden Council was divided, but a minority, including Lady Plowden herself, included a note of dissent which advocated fees for all children below the statutory starting age—i.e. the rising-fives and four-year-olds, as well as those in nursery schools and classes.[16]

The 1944 Education Act specifically forbids the charging of fees in maintained schools (Section 61) and would require amendment if they were to be introduced. There are two major arguments against fees.

First, even with a remission scheme, which would necessarily have to be a feature of any scheme, they would have a considerable deterrent effect on large numbers of families who would just fail to qualify for remission. These are not the poorest families, but they are only one step above poverty and many of the children who need nursery education most would be found among them. Secondly, it would add one more to the over forty means-tested benefits which together hold upwards of a million families in a vice-like poverty trap. Each wage increase merely reduces the means-tested benefits available and is immediately cancelled out.

These two objections to fees reinforce the principle on which our education system has worked for many years, that all education in maintained schools should be free. One of the most welcome educational developments in recent years has been the large numbers of pupils staying on at school after the statutory leaving age. In 1971 49 per cent remained at school after their fifteenth birthday in the maintained schools. No fees are charged for this large and growing group outside the statutory period of school life because of the deterrent effect they would have, indeed maintenance grants are available to encourage staying on. The argument against fees is equally strong, perhaps stronger, in the pre-school years.

Apart from these substantial objections the mechanics of fee-collecting and the operating of remissions would be extremely difficult. There would also be a number of very difficult questions of equity as between one group and another to be settled: for example, if the four-year-old in the nursery class pays, should the four-year-old, or the rising-five, in the primary school also pay? After all they are often in the same school.

The running costs of a nursery school and a nursery class are estimated in this plan at £250 and £150 for full-time places respectively. On the basis of a 40-week year, fees which aimed at covering the cost would have to be in the region of £2.50 per week, at 1971 prices, for half-time attendance. A fee of this kind would be impossible for large numbers of families, and remissions would have to be so widespread as to make the scheme rather ridiculous.

Added to the social and educational objections, as well as the practical difficulties involved, there would be considerable public objection to an erosion of the principle that schooling has long been free and that the best interests of the majority of people are served by keeping it free. This would be reflected in intense political opposition of the kind seen in recent years when free milk was withdrawn from primary schools and when the government announced its intention to charge the full cost for school meals. And the government has learnt its lesson—no fees are proposed in the White Paper.[36]

In Chapter 5 the case for pre-school education was summarized, and its importance in compensating for the effects of deprivation—particularly multiple deprivation—was stressed. This is a major part of the case for it, though not the whole case by any means. Because of this, any plan aimed at universal provision must begin by providing places in areas where deprivation is concentrated, and it is proposed that the five-years plan should first satisfy the demand in these areas before it makes places available more generally—i.e. there must initially be positive discrimination in favour of educational priority areas.

The concept of the educational priority area as an area "where educational handicaps are reinforced by social handicaps" was developed by the Plowden Report, which recommended positive discrimination in order to help areas of this kind.[16] It also advocated objective criteria to define such areas, and to assess the additional help to be given to them. There are considerable problems about finding criteria which will include inner city areas of the older industrial towns and, at the same time, small run-down industrial communities in such areas as the West Riding, Durham and Cumberland. There are also problems of quantifying and standardizing the factors chosen, as well as weighting them in order to roll them all up in one index. Dr Halsey has pointed out recently that no system of weighting is likely to be suitable for every local area.[31]

The Plowden criteria were:

social class composition
family size
overcrowding
supplements from the State
poor school attendance and truancy
children unable to speak English
retarded, disturbed and handicapped pupils in schools
incomplete families.

A DES circular in 1967 (11/67) put forward two general criteria:

multiple deprivation in the environment, such as above-average family size and overcrowding
general quality of the environment, such as large numbers of substandard houses.

The problem of delineating these areas has not yet been solved. The Labour Government in the first phase of the Urban Aid Programme used two criteria—overcrowding and density of immigrants. This inadequate definition which, for example, excluded the city of Leeds, was abandoned for the second phase where local authorities were merely asked to submit their own bids and—so far as the education element was concerned—DES used its own resources to select a programme from the submissions.

The index developed by the Inner London Education Authority is by far the most viable attempt at definition so far, but to be universally applicable it would need to incorporate a factor which assessed the economic prospects of the area, though of course a number of other criteria, such as sub-standard housing, are related to economic prospects. This factor illustrates the need for regionally flexible weighting; for example, a depressed mining village in North-West Durham would base its major claim to being a priority area on the decline in coal mining and the shortage of other employment, with all the social and environmental consequences which follow.

There is urgent need for a pooling of experience by local authorities on the definition of education priority areas. From their experience it should be possible to agree on a reasonably comprehensive definition which still allows for the exceptions.

Having defined the area, it is important to remember that it is nothing more than a framework within which a policy of positive discrimination in the allocation of resources is to be applied. Not every child in most EP areas will be deprived and not every deprived child will be in a designated area. It is a blunt application of the policy to give a whole area priority in pre-school provision, but it is, of course, administratively essential to do this initially. It must, however, be accompanied by much more sophisticated attempts, both within education priority areas and outside them, to distinguish the deprived families and children, for they, and not the geographical area, are the ultimate units of deprivation.

To advocate, as this plan does, that say the first two years of a five-year plan should be devoted entirely to education priority areas is merely to cast the net in such a way that it will catch the worst concentrations of deprivation first. But many deprived children will be left out.

To focus the positive discrimination more accurately, and therefore to allocate resources more rationally, will call for imaginative new inter-departmental arrangements within local education authority areas going far beyond the education service, which it is not the purpose of this book to discuss. Dr Halsey's report on a Government-sponsored project to examine educational priority area policy outlines a possible approach.[31] There is also a good deal to be learnt from the Head Start programme in the United States in the assembling of a battery of services at pre-school centres.

8. Nursery Class

The nursery school is defined by the Department of Education and Science as a county or voluntary primary school used mainly for providing education for children who have reached the age of two, but are under five. In practice two-year-olds are rarely admitted.[42] In January 1971 there were only 646 two-year-olds in all maintained schools. In some local authority areas such as the West Riding most of the children in the nursery schools are four years of age. There are also many privately owned schools and classes which cater for pre-school children and call themselves "nursery schools."

A nursery class in a county primary school or voluntary primary school is mainly for children who are over three but under five. In each case the word "mainly" is used to permit children to stay on in the nursery until the end of the term in which they reach their fifth birthday. Most of the places provided under the Urban Aid Programme are in nursery classes, and 96 per cent of the expansion proposed in Chapter 7 would be in the classes of this kind. There is a great deal to be said for having the nursery in the same building as the Infant School for ease of transition from one to the other, provided the accommodation is adapted for pre-school children and this usually involves considerable capital expenditure, as it includes such items as direct access to the outdoor playing space and the provision of indoor toilets. The cost per place provided in this way is however less than in a new nursery school. (See page 96.)

The Department of Education and Science has laid down quite detailed regulations which local authorities should observe when providing nursery places.[42] The site of a nursery school must be not less than a quarter of an acre for not more than 40 children, with an additional one-eighth acre for every additional 20 children. Similarly, if a nursery class is provided in a primary school, the site of the school must be increased by these amounts, though, clearly, this regulation is not being observed by some local authorities or enforced by DES, e.g. where a nursery class is established in an older Infant School in an inner city area it will rarely be possible to extend the site.

There is an imaginative regulation that every nursery school and class must have as part of its site a garden playing space of at least 100 sq ft per child, and of this 40 sq ft should have an impervious surface such as tar macadam, concrete or flags. Inside the school or class there must be play space of at least 25 sq ft per child. These two regulations could provide yardsticks for social service departments in deciding on their requirements when granting certificates of registration to play-groups. (See page 120.)

There are equally explicit regulations about storage space; facilities for drying clothing, washing and sanitary arrangements (one wash-basin and one toilet for every ten children); storage space for apparatus, equipment, beds and large toys; kitchen accommodation, etc.

The school day is defined as "... at least three hours of suitable activities," with half this period when the children attend for half a day. Most schools and classes, in fact, have sessions of $2\frac{1}{2}$ hours in the morning and 2 hours in the afternoon.

Staffing requirements are that each nursery school shall have a superintendent teacher in charge assisted by "... a staff of assistant teachers suitable and sufficient in number to provide education appropriate to the ages and aptitudes of the pupils."[42] With the expansion of nursery education since the Urban Aid Programme started in 1969 there is already a shortage of teachers specifically trained as nursery teachers. Forty-six Colleges of Education provided courses in nursery teaching as a main subject in 1972, but if there is to be a rapid expansion of nursery education in the remaining years of the present decade, training facilities must be provided on a much wider scale than this. The present pupil/teacher ratio in maintained nurseries is 35 : 1 although the ratio of pupils to teachers and nursery assistants is 13 : 1. Clearly the ratio of teachers to nursery assistants is too low, and the teaching profession as well as interested parents will demand an improvement. Assuming that a pupil/teacher ratio of 25 : 1 is the goal, the expansion programme proposed in Chapter 7 would require an additional 13,000 teachers over the five years, which is considerably more than the output of the present courses.

In addition to a qualified teacher, each nursery class will have at least one, and in most cases two, nursery assistants, who will probably have undergone a two-year work-based training course at a College of Further Education under a scheme of training approved by The National Nursery Examination Board (NNEB). In 1970 2,956 students sat for the Board's examination in England and Wales. This was an increase of 11 per cent over 1969. The Board, in addition to administering the final examination, lays down entry requirements and provides a syllabus to guide the colleges in arranging their courses.

The age of entry is normally sixteen, although there are now shorter courses for mature students over twenty-five who have at least three years' experience of the group care of children. The training itself is the joint responsibility of the college and the school or other establishment in which the student is based. This may be a nursery or infant school, or a day or residential nursery. After training the student may seek work in any institution involving the group care of children.

The Plowden Report made a number of recommendations for improving the training, status, pay and career prospects of nursery assistants.[16] It was suggested that a nursery assistant should be in charge of the "day-to-day work" of a nursery group of 20 children. Up to three groups (i.e. 60 children) were to be under the "ultimate supervision" of a qualified teacher—a proposal which was reminiscent of the Monitorial System of Bell and Lancaster in the 19th century. (See page 74.)

Since Plowden (1967) teacher supply generally has improved considerably. In the early '70s, upwards of 20,000 additional teachers have been available each year. At the same time the rapid rise in the number of pupils in maintained schools which had taken place each year since 1960 began to slacken. As a result pupil/teacher ratios have dropped to all-time low levels.

In the face of this there does not appear to be any reason why the Plowden expedient should be adopted. It now makes much more sense to increase the number of qualified teachers in the nursery schools and reduce the ratio of nursery assistants to teachers, though of course many more will be required, but the present rate of growth of students taking NNEB courses appears to be adequate. If hybrid groupings of both local authority nurseries and independent playgroups are to emerge, the trained nursery teacher will have important advisory functions in addition to teaching. This development also will require a greater proportion of teachers.

Although the Colleges of Further Education have taken great pride in their courses for nursery assistants, the educational content of their work is of such importance that their training could be more effectively undertaken in the Colleges of Education where the greatest concentrations of teacher training skills are to be found. It would also improve understanding if nursery teachers and nursery assistants who are going to work together in the same classroom could learn their professions in the same institution. There would also be advantages in the use of libraries and other facilities in the Colleges of Education.

This proposal, together with the similar one to train playgroup leaders where possible in the Colleges of Education, would inject a small but much needed degree of variety into the Colleges. Their present monotechnic nature is one of their less desirable features.

Having outlined the regulations which govern local authority nurseries we now turn to look at a typical nursery class attached to an Infant School on Tyneside. It has thirty children aged three and four. The staff consists of one qualified teacher, and two nursery assistants. There is also one trainee nursery assistant undertaking a course at the local college. All the children attend full-time from 9 a.m. to 3.30 p.m., and most stay for lunch.

One nursery assistant begins her day at 8.30 and ends at 3.15. The other begins at 9 and stays after school until the last child has been collected by his mother, and with so many working mothers this may be considerably later than 3.30. Local authorities must make this arrangement if part-time nursery education is to become universally available.

The assistant who is on early duty prepares the nursery for the busy day which lies ahead. She will mix the paint, put it out and erect the easels; mix dough or clay; put out table games and materials; open the house corner and the book shelves; set up climbing apparatus, etc. Some of the activity materials provided vary from day to day, but there is a great deal of careful planning by the teacher of what is available each day. The aim is to provide in due order all the play materials which are needed for the stages of development reached and meticulous records are kept. This is the expert organizational basis behind the nursery where the children "play all day." There are some activities of course which are so basic that they are available all the time; for example, the home corner, the book corner, bricks and boxes of all kinds, painting, etc. The teacher arrives at 8.45, supervises the preparation and ensures that all is ready by 9 a.m.

When the children arrive they are welcomed by the teacher and her two assistants. Mothers are talked to, and every day there are problems to be mentioned or discussed. Equally important, the children, bursting with information they want to pass on, are listened to. Eventually they settle down to their activities, the teacher and her two assistants each supervising a group of ten.

Part of each morning is devoted to a special activity, such as making things from papier-mâché, collage-arranging using a wide variety of materials, baking, making and using puppets, box craft, tie-and-dye, etc. This may involve one or more of the groups of ten. Another group will be outside if the weather is fine, with outdoor toys and climbing apparatus, gardening, kite-flying, shopping or visiting the local park. Before lunch there will also be singing, dancing, playing musical instruments, mime or story-telling.

None of the activities will be compulsory. If a child wants to keep on painting or building a castle from egg-boxes, or looking at books, instead of listening to a story or dancing, he is free to do so if, of course, the preparations for lunch allow it. After all no mother would insist that her child must do the things *she* wanted him to do throughout the day in the home, and the good home is a good guide for the nursery teacher.

Each of the groups will have five minutes in the bathroom with the teacher or assistant before lunch. At lunch all four staff sit with the children and serve them. This is a useful opportunity for relaxed, uninhibited conversation. The school—any school—with the silent dining hall, apart from being guilty of sheer cruelty for its own convenience, is missing an uniquely valuable opportunity for language development —which after all is a major purpose of education.

After lunch the children, rather sleepy now, settle down for a quiet period on the carpets in the nursery. Some play quietly; some listen to a story; others nod off to sleep. They are supervised by the teacher and one assistant while the other prepares the materials for the afternoon. The staff take their own midday break in turn, but by 1.15 the activities are all in full swing again. They may include games such as lotto, dominoes, matching, sorting, pre-reading games, colour games, etc. At 1.45 the radio programme "Listen with Mother" is available on the radio. Here again they may listen or not as they wish.

By 2.15 all the staff are again available and, weather permitting, a large group may be taken out into the school field, where there are endless possibilities for activities, games, and conversation—and it is amazing how much excitement is aroused by the sight of a worm, a snail or a butterfly. Half an hour later, and very much more tired, most children will be attracted by a nature talk, feeding the pets, or a simple story.

Milk and biscuits are now available with each group sitting around informally on the floor rather than at their tables, talking about the news and generally discussing the happenings of the day in the nursery—always an exciting and fertile source of conversation for young children. While this is going on mothers begin to arrive, but the period of departure may last until 4 p.m. or later.

During the day the trainee assistant helps in the preparation of games and activities, with the undressing and dressing, in the bathroom, at lunch time, in putting the material away, washing brushes, etc. From time to time she looks after a group of children, and throughout the day uses every chance she gets to talk with them, observe them and record her observations.

Throughout the year there are a great many special events, such as those associated with the religious festivals, including the harvest festival, summer outings, visits to such places as the local fire station or clinic, birthday parties (these days provide an opportunity for a baking session!), Halloween (making turnip lanterns), St Valentine's Day, Mothering Sunday, Sports day with the Infant School children, etc.

A school day organized in this way is a sensible compromise between a wholly structured and wholly unstructured day. The rich variety of activities which the ingenuity and hard work of the staff have provided and for which they have assembled an astonishing range of materials is available throughout. Sometimes everyone is involved in them. At other times only the occasional child, while the rest are engaged in a special activity.

The day is punctuated by special activities which may attract a whole group or the whole class, in which the children are encouraged but not compelled to join. The teacher takes the view that the constraints which mere attendance at the nursery class—being among other children, not always getting his own way, etc.—places upon a three-year-old, are a sufficient initial instalment of the "shades of the prison house" without also imposing on him a strict timetable to which he must conform. Her aim is to give the greatest possible degree of freedom of choice to each child compatible with a reasonably orderly daily routine. And children themselves feel more secure when there is a regular routine——provided the routine does not become more important than their enjoyment and well-being.

A nursery of this kind can provide well supervised care by trained and skilled adults who become known, relied upon, and—one hopes—loved. A context of care and love is the prerequisite of security—security in which confidence, skill, intellect, emotional control, and social grace can grow.

Whatever the degree of structuring, i.e. having a timetable which divides the day into separate activities, there should never be any sitting down in a class to learn in a formal manner. The nursery teacher who tries to "get her children on" is doing the job of her Infant School colleague. The aim of the nursery school is to supplement the educational and social influence of the good home and, unfortunately in some cases, to compensate for the shortcomings of the less satisfactory home. In the development of children there is a time for everything and for the great majority the time for reading, writing and learning to manipulate numbers is not at the age of three or four. Nor must the teacher expect and demand an end-product from the child's play with paint, dough, clay, etc. The important thing is for him to experiment and explore, not to produce something to exhibit on the wall or take home to mother. He may do that of course, and delight in his achievement, but he should not be *expected* to do it.

Excellent though most of our local authority nursery schools and classes are they too often lack the one dimension which could greatly increase their effectiveness—parental involvement. The Douglas Reports[12, 44] and other studies have demonstrated the importance of the attitude of the home in the achievements of children in school. Indeed this was the message of Pestalozzi a century and a half ago. (See page 77.) But we still have not accepted it. With very young children the need for the closest contacts between home and school is all the more important both for the children who need the interest of their parents, and for the parents who need the advice and help of the school in the educational aspects of bringing up their children.

The playgroup movement has been pre-eminently successful in involving parents; not merely in retaining their interest, but in sharing the task of educating their children. In this way many playgroups have made themselves into valuable community centres of interest in education, which benefits education generally as well as the playgroups. Of course, by its very nature, the playgroup is in most cases a parents' co-operative, but the rota of mothers who act as helpers is one aspect which could well be adopted by local authority nurseries. Similarly the mothers' club of the kind associated with some of the groups would be an invaluable adjunct to a nursery school or class. Most nurseries allow mothers to stay to help their children off with their coats and very often to see them started on the day's occupations. Many invite them into the school regularly to see it functioning, as well as to special occasions such as the Christmas Party or Harvest Festival. Others invite groups of mothers and fathers to help in making equipment. A parent-teacher organization may help if it does not degenerate into a formal meeting once a month attended by frustrated parents and reluctant teachers.

All these are steps in the right direction, but we should now go much further and invite mothers to participate in the actual running of the nurseries as voluntary assistants on a rota basis. Also the nurseries could copy the playgroups in their attitude to *parental* education, which should be as important as the education of the children; indeed educating mothers is the best way of educating their children. This means giving advice, both individually and to groups of parents, on problems often terrifying to the young mother, concerning the intellectual development of their children. Of these, those about language development are by far the most important.

The selection of books and toys which are appropriate to the age of the child, which will give him the right kind of stimulus at the right time calls for expert knowledge which the trained teacher can give. The school bookshop was mentioned in Chapter 3. It would be of very great help to parents if a bookstall could be available in every school for certain periods each week. And it would be even more valuable if appropriate toys could also be on sale or at least on exhibition. There is no need to start a commercial enterprise in competition with the local shopkeepers. All the material on sale could be obtained on a sale-or-return basis.

In view of all we have learnt in recent years about the importance of the parent as the child's principal teacher and about the need to integrate education with the community in which it takes place, the time has now come for the teachers' professional organizations to rethink their attitudes towards parental involvement in the classroom. Their fears in the past were understandable, but today they are less credible and very much outweighed by the gain which would accrue to the teachers themselves and to education generally.

9. Playgroup

Privately organized nursery groups had existed, here and there throughout the first half of this century, including some notably successful ones in slum areas, but it was not until after World War II that the idea of a parental co-operative providing nursery education really caught on. There was a considerable demand for nursery schools in the 1950s, which local education authorities were quite unable to satisfy because of shortages of money, teachers and buildings. A rapidly growing school population, and the enormous backlog of building from the war years added to their difficulties. Virtually no additional resources could be found for nursery education.

At the same time, married women were coming to regard it as normal that they should keep their jobs after marriage. This was probably partly due to their wartime experience of running a home and also doing a job outside, and partly a result of rising living standards. Many women went out to work at least initially with a number of material targets in mind—a washing machine, refrigerator, television or car, but eventually the additional income in the family became a necessity. Whatever the reason, the working mother discovered she often had a problem about the day care of her pre-school children. In fairness to working mothers, it is also true that the period since the war has seen a quite remarkable growth of interest in, and knowledge about, education in all social classes.

In these circumstances it was not surprising that there should be a good deal of campaigning for nursery schools. In the early '50s middle-class mothers became increasingly articulate in their demands to local and central government but by the early '60s the campaign involved a wide social cross-section of the nation. During the 1961 campaign the following letter was printed in *The Guardian* on the 25th August:

Do-it-yourself Nurseries

To the rescue of Margaret Hughes ("Baby at the centre," July 28) and other mothers desperate about the lack of facilities for children under five, comes a newly formed organization, with a do-it-yourself spirit, The Nursery School Campaign.

Beginning as a local effort in St. Marylebone, it has now extended to anyone, mother or teacher, who is concerned about the dismal situation at present and the equally dismal future, and is steadily gaining support not only in London but in many parts of the north and midlands.

The campaign has two aims.

To gather names for a large scale national petition to be presented to the Minister of Education, asking him for more nursery schools and play facilities for children under five.

The other is to encourage groups of mothers to start their own schools wherever they can find suitable premises employing trained teachers especially those who are married with their own small children and who want only part-time jobs.

The campaign has received considerable advice and encouragement from the Nursery School Association, The Save the Children Fund and the Advisory Centre on Education, and many of its members come from the Housebound Housewives Register.

Enquiries are welcomed (particularly those enclosing a stamped and addressed envelope) from mothers and teachers who would like to create their own solutions to their problems.

Yours etc.

(Mrs) B. Tutaev.

There was an immediate response to Belle Tutaev's offer to give advice. Mothers wrote to her in large numbers. Playgroups mushroomed throughout the country. By personal contact successful groups encouraged others to start, and the foundation members often began to function as voluntary organizers for their areas. A great deal of the success of the movement is due to their dedication. Some local education authorities started to take an interest in the new groups and occasionally to give some financial help, but more often to give valuable advice, and the local health authority had to approve the premises used and the suitability of the group leaders.

The Pre-School Playgroups Association was formed in 1962 as a charity, and has been a roaring success ever since. At its Annual Meeting in Birmingham in 1963 an Area Organizer scheme was initiated and a code of standards agreed for approved groups. The following year the area organizers held their first conference. In 1966 the Department of Education and Science gave its first grant to enable a National Organizer to be appointed. By then the membership was 1,300 and the annual income £2,200. The same year saw the Association's excellent magazine *Contact* under the editorship of Kate Moodie. *Contact* is a major instrument for the interchange of ideas and the dissemination of information throughout the Association—and in a movement of this kind the free flow of ideas is its very life-blood.

In 1967 Brenda Crowe, a highly experienced nursery school teacher, was appointed National Adviser and Dr W. D. Wall became the President. A year later a Scottish Pre-School Playgroups Association was formed. In 1969 Mary Bruce was appointed General Secretary. Mrs Bruce, Mrs Crowe and Dr Wall have guided the movement through these early years with missionary zeal tempered with good sense and considerable administrative skill.

In 1971/72 the Association received a grant of £7,000 from the Department of Education and Science to make possible the appointment of an additional national adviser, £1,000 from the National Playing Fields Association and £3,000 from the Joseph Rowntree Social Services Trust. Help was being given by 44 local authorities in England and Wales and 13 in Scotland to PPA branches and playgroups. These now range from grants of £5,000 from the Inner London Education Authority and £9,000 from Wandsworth and Glasgow to the appointment of advisers by a number of authorities.

Today there are 150 branches, in which there are playgroups catering for 200,000 children.

It is a remarkable story of dedication, enthusiasm and growth. Its most significant achievement has been to involve mothers in the education of their children to an extent never previously achieved either inside or outside the maintained schools. If the playgroup movement ceased to exist tomorrow it would have made a considerable contribution to the education of young children and, equally important, of their mothers.

The term "playgroup" usually means a group of children who are meeting regularly under a leader to play in premises approved for the purpose by the Social Services Department of the local authority. Nothing more can be assumed from the name "playgroup." Groups vary a great deal from some which are at least the equal of the maintained nursery class to some which are little more than devices for child-minding. Although the local authority can insist on its requirement regarding the premises and the general fitness of the people who are to run the groups, it has inadequate power to inspect them from an educational point of view, although some local authorities give a considerable amount of educational advice.

The better group will function in premises which are bright, clean, warm, large enough for the more massive activities and have suitable play-space out of doors, including a garden. Control of the group will be in the hands of a committee of parents. A study of twenty playgroups in Southwark by the National Children's Bureau found that only nine groups had committees and that of these eight included mothers as about half of their membership.[40] They will select the leader, raise money to purchase equipment, decide the fees to be charged, and the nature and financing of a scheme for remission of fees where the need arises. The group will have accumulated a large and varied amount of the kind of material and equipment mentioned in Chapter 2, much of which will of necessity have to be improvised from scrap material—and it will be all the better for that. It will be a happy place where the three- and four-year-old children are constantly absorbed, where there is always something to interest them, where they feel secure. They will enjoy music, singing and story-telling, beautiful sounds, things and materials; activities to exercise one of the young child's greatest gifts—his sense of wonder; others to stimulate him to find out and discover things for himself. Fees will probably be about 15p. for each session (1972), though in most groups there will be provision for remission in cases of need. The remission scheme may be financed from local authority grants, from special fund-raising efforts or from the fees paid by other children. In the groups proposed to be recognized under the expansion plan in Chapter 7 a scheme of this kind would be an essential feature.

The group leader will probably, and preferably, be a mother who may or may not have had professional training as a teacher, a nurse or a nursery assistant. In any case she will almost certainly have attended a course for playgroup leaders meeting once or twice a week at the local

College of Further Education or College of Education for a year. When the group is first established it will in many cases be impossible to find a leader who has completed or indeed started, a leaders' course. In these circumstances it is highly desirable for the leader-elect to begin the course and at least complete about half of it before the group begins to operate. She should also during this few months of preparation visit as many other established groups, nursery schools and classes as possible. Before she begins all this she may imagine that there is nothing much to it—that any sensible, pleasant mum could run a group competently. But the more she learns the more she will realize there is to learn?!

Reading is another part of the leader's training. The Pre-School Playgroups Association has an excellent and growing list of publications which are reasonably priced and are essential reading for every leader and committee member. The magazine *Contact,* as its name implies, is a major agent for the cross-fertilization of ideas throughout the movement in the country. It is to be hoped that the potential leader will also read much wider than this and there is a growing literature on the education of young children.

The experience of the past ten years has shown that the professionally trained leader appears to have no special advantage over the untrained mother as a playgroup leader, unless she has been trained as a nursery school teacher, but that the leaders' course is of help to both.

"Even good teachers have acknowledged the help that they needed before understanding the extra dimension of mother involvement in playgroup work."[44]

The leader will probably have an assistant leader who may or may not have attended a leaders' course. In the well-run group with a high degree of parental involvement there will also be a rota of mothers who will act as ancillary helpers. In the Southwark survey, eleven of the twenty groups had rotas and 62 per cent of the mothers with children in the groups took a share in the duty.[40] The leader and her assistant may be paid a small salary which will vary considerably from one group to another, but would probably be £1.50 and £1 respectively per session (1972). On the whole it is preferable to have paid leaders. They frequently have additional domestic expenses because of their playgroup activities, but in addition their relationship with the committee is much more business-like than it is when they are entirely voluntary workers.

Of course in a voluntary movement as extensive as this not all groups reach this standard of premises, equipment or calibre of leader. Indeed some are not connected with the Pre-School Playgroups Association or any other national organization, and are unaffected by all their efforts to maintain and raise standards. Some meet in homes and have the merit of an atmosphere which closely resembles the children's own homes. But these also vary a good deal.

At one extreme they merge into child-minding—particularly as they are often run by individuals and not by committees; on the other hand they can be among the most attractive forms of nursery education, with their small numbers, their homely context and all the domestic facilities available to them.

Other groups meet in hired premises such as a Church Hall, but are privately run, without a committee, for profit and the fees may be quite high—25p. a half-day session would not be unusual. Here again the standard varies. In some cases a group will be run by a trained teacher; in others by an untrained lady whose main motive may be to help the children and the parents in the area, or it may be merely to provide herself with an income. Privately run groups usually do not involve parents. Thus they lack the major virtue of the pre-school playgroups. If to this is added a completely untrained leader who is outside the influence of the Pre-School Playgroups Association, they are not a credible type of nursery education. If the playgroup is to have a permanent place in our pre-school pattern as proposed in Chapter 7 it will be necessary to provide some device to protect the consumer in this field. An obvious way of doing this would be to give the local education authority powers of inspection, in place of or in addition to those which the Social Services Department now possess, with a licensing requirement which involved the approval on both educational and health grounds.

Playgroups of the co-operative type come into existence in a variety of ways, but the most common initiative would be an informal discussion among a few mothers often exasperated at the failure of the local authority to provide nursery places. This could be followed by a more formal meeting of mothers and probably fathers too, at which a decision to form a group would be made. The Pre-School Playgroups Association would almost certainly be asked for advice, and would give it freely. (See list of addresses, page 127.) Committee members and potential leaders would also, one hopes, visit as many existing groups and nursery schools as possible. This is particularly important.

Other groups are formed as an additional activity of another organization such as a tenants' association, church, or Women's Institute branch. This type of group usually has an initial advantage in its more extensive contacts, sounder finances, and in the availability of premises. Its weakness often is that the group is controlled by the sponsoring organization and not by a committee of parents. It cannot be overstressed that if playgroups do not involve the parents of their children in both their management and running, their claim to be a permanent part of our pre-school provision is greatly weakened.

There is a third way in which groups may start—by local authority initiative. In areas of multiple deprivation where the need is greatest, this may be the only way. The group is usually in premises and with equipment provided by the local authority. The mothers, selected by local authority social workers, are invited to take their children. A more effective way suggested by Brenda Crowe is to begin with a Mothers' Club.[44] While the mothers are meeting for a cup of tea and a chat some arrangement has to be made for their young children, and out of this arrangement a playgroup emerges. Getting a leader without importing a well-meaning do-gooder is a problem in areas of this kind but eventually, with help and advice, mothers usually do emerge who are capable of becoming excellent leaders. They need confidence in themselves in order to take on this kind of responsibility. In the meantime the social worker's good sense and understanding will hold the two groups, of parents and children, together.

In deprived areas there is often a high concentration of immigrants and their need for pre-school facilities for their children is very great indeed. Added to the multiple deprivation of the area in which they are forced to live, they have a considerable language problem. Their mothers usually know only their native language. But a strange language is only part of the alien culture into which they are thrown when the children enter the Infant School. The small well-run playgroup can help them to acquire and use their new language but, more important, it can establish close and reassuring relationships with the adults who run the group and when this happens the alien culture will become a more attractive one and one which gives confidence and security. Of course great sensitivity is needed in such matters as religion, dress, and social customs. The important point is not to break the old continuities in the child's life—or the parents'. Respect their culture, customs and creeds. Parents may show an excessive, sometimes obsessive, desire to conform to the norms of their new communities, but this is because it is usually believed by them to be the most helpful attitude to adopt to prevent any handicap to their children. In spite of this there will be greater co-operation with the group leader who does not demand conformity but who respects, and indeed uses, the cultural background of her immigrant children, e.g. their songs, dances and dress, to enrich the activities of her group.

Parental involvement may be an uphill task in the multi-racial group—because of shyness, or language, or because the views of immigrant parents from Commonwealth countries about education may still be based on the martinet schoolmasters who flourished under the British Raj who, to say the least, discouraged parents from assuming that education was any business of theirs. But once the initial reserve has been overcome the gain to parents and their children can be enormous.

All groups must obtain a certificate of registration from the Social Services Department of the Local Authority under Section 3 of the Nurseries and Childminders Act, 1948 *before* opening. The Act as amended on a number of occasions since 1948 lays upon a local authority the duty to keep a register of the premises other than private dwellings—where children are received to be looked after for two hours or over and "of persons who for reward receive into their homes children under the age of five to be looked after . . . ." It gives the power to refuse registration if they are not satisfied that the premises are suitable, or the person who is seeking registration or anyone who is to be employed by him in looking after the children is not a fit person to look after children. This gives extremely wide discretion which is reinforced by the power to make requirements which must be set out in the certificate of registration. It goes further still by naming some requirements which may be attached to registration. The number of children permitted may be stated and specific precautions against infectious diseases may be required. Equally important, it may lay down the number, qualifications and experience of the staff to be employed as well as the ratio of adults to children. It may also impose requirements to ensure that the equipment is adequate, that both equipment and premises are properly maintained, that feeding arrangements are made and that the children are under adequate medical supervision. Of particular value is the power to require records of the children to be kept and these must contain whatever particulars the local authority specifies.

These are extremely wide powers, which have not been fully used by a great many local authorities—some of whom are still heard to complain about the quality of playgroups in their areas. A more rigorous use of the Act, coupled with some financial and advisory aid, could raise the whole standard of playgroups enormously throughout the country.

The power of inspection is also wide—though it could be wider and more specific in giving power to examine and report on the educational standards of the groups. Nevertheless it does give a right of entry at all reasonable times to inspect the premises *and* the children, the arrangements for their welfare *and* any records which the group may have been required to keep. These powers added to those concerning equipment are wider than is popularly supposed in giving the local authority more control over the educational standards of the groups.

As well as registration, which is, of course, compulsory, the wise group committee will register as a charity. Also even in the best-run group with the most able leader there is, unfortunately, always the possibility of accidents and insurance is essential. The Pre-School Playgroups Association can offer a policy specially designed for this purpose. It would be a very ill-advised committee which did not provide insurance cover of at least £50,000 to £75,000. The value of money is falling at a rate which makes an annual review of the cover an essential item of business on the agenda of every annual meeting, particularly in the light of any Court awards made during the year.

The committee must be businesslike about finance if the stability of the group is to be assured. If the number of children per session is to be limited to a maximum of twenty-four, as it should be, and if the payments to the leader and her assistant are approximately £2.50, the fee paid by each child must be at least 10p. each session to cover this item alone. But there are other considerable expenses, such as rent which may not include lighting, heating and cleaning, the replacement of expendable equipment—and it is amazing how much paper, paint, paste, etc., young children can use in three hours, toilet materials, mid-morning snacks—and a scheme for remission of fees in cases of need.

Fees paid at present (1972) vary from 5p. to 50p. Those of Save the Children Fund groups tend to be the lowest. A condition of local authority financial assistance may be that the fees are kept within a stated range. They should be sufficient for the group to run without cutting down on essentials, but not so high that they deter the poorer parent who is not poor enough to qualify for remission. In higher income areas in the suburbs this will present little difficulty, but in the areas of urban decay in some older cities and some of the old run-down industrial communities, the money is harder to find to run a successful group without financial help from the local authority. That is why it was proposed in Chapter 7 that recurrent grants should be available to groups in educational priority areas as well as capital grants when the groups are started.

In both the financially viable group and the one with an acute financial problem, there is a great deal to be said for the committee raising funds in addition to the income from fees. This is essential for the purchase of initial equipment, but it is equally important when the group is functioning—not least because it gives the parents an additional sense of responsibility for their group.

And parental involvement is the *sine qua non* of the playgroup. It is important for two reasons. First, the group is a better group if the parents of its children are heavily involved in both supporting and running it. But, second, regular contact with the example of a successful playgroup gives confidence, comfort and help to mothers, especially those who are young and inexperienced in bringing up their own children. Educating the mother is as much a function of a playgroup as educating her child. Chapter 3 discussed the colossal task which every mother has to face of teaching her child his native language. This is an example of an aspect of child-rearing where mothers could learn a great deal which would be of direct value to their children. The value of introducing educational material into the home has been seen in the Home Visiting Programme in the West Riding.[31] This scheme involves mothers *before* their children join the playgroup, but it demonstrates the value of teaching the mother how to teach her child and she, after all, is his principal teacher. In her close association with the playgroup she will learn a great deal about how children learn and she will have frequent opportunities to discuss her problems with other mothers.

Apart from serving on the committee and on the rota, working in fund-raising efforts and undertaking *ad hoc* tasks, e.g. decorating or making equipment for the group, a good deal more can be done to involve and help parents. A weekly bookstall in the hall where the group meets, or even in the market-place, helps parents to obtain appropriate educational material—particularly story books. Occasional discussion groups of parents with a discussion leader from the local authority, the Pre-School Playgroups Association, or the local nursery school, will reduce parental problems to their correct perspective and help many worried and over-anxious mothers *and* fathers. A wide distribution of *Contact* among the parents of a group would be extremely useful—particularly if the discussions could sometimes be centred on its contents. To improve the quality of mothering should be a major function of a playgroup.

The group will function in much the same way as the nursery class which was described in the last chapter. The leader and her assistant will arrive twenty minutes before the children and, by the time they turn up a variety of materials for play activities will be out, and ready for them. There should be a choice of upwards of twenty different things to do, ranging from the basic activity of playing with bricks or Lego to tasks involving a number of skills, such as model-making which needs cutting, pasting and painting.

There will be freedom to choose and change activities at will, without fussy attempts by the leader to "suggest" what Peter or Sarah should do. Even group activities such as listening to a story or making music should be quite voluntary. Discipline is a pompous word at the best of times, but applied to three- or four-year-olds it is rather terrifying. However, some rules are needed and are quickly accepted. In the group they soon understand that no one can enjoy what he is doing unless everyone restrains himself to some extent. This is the beginning of self-discipline.

This free, unstructured session is the ideal—but a difficult one to organize without it sliding into chaos. The secret is to reconcile the organization of a wide range of activities with a leader posture which is unobtrusive, but ever-present, which is constantly helping and caring, but never self-apologetic.

Some leaders, like some nursery teachers, fully structure each session. Some cannot manage their groups unless they do. A common pattern is made up of a period for free activities followed by a few minutes of putting all the equipment and material away. Next comes the mid-session drink of milk or fruit juice. The session is then rounded off with story-telling or singing and movement for everyone. All that remains is to make sure that everyone is dressed for the mothers who descend on the group towards the end of the session.

It is quite impossible to generalize about which is the most effective approach—unstructured, fully structured or a compromise between the two. Most new leaders probably need to start with a loosely structured programme if only for the disciplinary effect of the change of activity *for everyone.* But, with more experience and knowledge it should be possible to abandon the structuring and allow freedom of choice of activity throughout the session but to do this before the leader has confidence in her ability to organize it and before the children have acquired some self-discipline is often to invite trouble.

References

1   *Working Class Mothers and Pre-School Education:* Newcastle Action Group: 1971.

2   *Children's Rights:* Elek Books: 1971.

3   *Pocket Book of Baby and Child Care:* New English Library: 1971.

4   *Mothercraft:* Simpkin, Marshall Ltd.: 1942: 8th Edn.

5   *The First Five Years of Life:* Methuen & Co. Ltd.: 1971.

6   *The Nursery Years:* Routledge & Kegan Paul Ltd.: 1971: (Pub. 1929).

7   *Education: Its Data and First Principles:* Edward Arnold & Co.: 1920.

8   *Children's Play:* Michael Joseph: 1970.

9   *Trident Magazine:* Autumn 1972.

10 Address by Prof. Eric Hawkins to BMA Reprinted in *Contact* from *Lancet:* 1971.

11 *Prime Minister's Committee on Higher Education* (Robbins Report): HMSO: 1963.

12 *The Home and the School:* McGibbon & Kee: 1964.

13 *Deprivation and Education:* Longman: 1971. 2nd Edn.

14 *The Plowden Children four years later:* NFRER: 1971.

15 Unpublished letter to the author.

16 *Children and their Primary Schools:* Central Advisory Council Report: HMSO: 1966.

17 *Voyage through Childhood into the Adult World:* Pergamon Press: 1967.

18 Paper to British Association for the Advancement of Science: 9.9.69.

19 *British Medical Journal:* 11.7.70.

20 *From Birth to Seven:* Longman: 1972.

21 *Intelligence and Cultural Environment:* Methuen: 1969.

22 *Harvard Educational Review:* June 1969.

23 Commissioned by the National Dairy Council: Reported Sept. 1970.

24 *Half our Future:* Central Advisory Council Report (England) HMSO: 1963.

25 Introduction to BBC TV Programme: 11.10.71 Repeated 21.8.72.

26 *Hansard.* Col. 735: 6.11.72.

27 *Education Psychology:* Pitman Education Library: 1972 (First published 1966 in Canada).

28 Dr John Bowlby: BBC TV Programme: 11.10.71. Repeated 21.8.72.

29 *Born Illegitimate:* NFER: 1971.

30 *The Trend of Reading Standards:* NFER: 1972.

31 *Educational Priority.* EPA Problems & Policies. Vol. 1.: HMSO: 1972.

32 *The Earliest Years:* Pergamon Educational Guides: 1966.

33 *Royal Commission on the State of Popular Education in England and Wales (1861):* (Newcastle Report).

34 *Consultative Committee on Infant and Primary Schools* (Hadow Report): 1933.

35 *Consultative Committee on School Attendance Below the Age of Five:* 1908.

36 *Education: A Framework for Expansion:* HMSO: 1972.

37 *The Illegal Child Minders:* Priority Area Children.

38 *A Fair Start—the Provision of Pre-School Education:* LSE Study: 1971.

39 *Children in Distress:* Penguin Educational Special: 1968.

40 *Playgroups in an Area of Social Need:* National Children's Bureau.

41 *Committee on Local Authority and Allied Personal Social Services:* HMSO: 1968.

42 *The New Law of Education* by Taylor and Saunders: Butterworths: 1971: 7th Ed.

43 *All Our Future:* Peter Davies: 1968.

44 *The Playgroup Movement:* PPA Publication: 1971.

Useful Addresses

Advisory Centre for Education   32 Trumpington Street, Cambridge CB2 1QY (Cambridge 51456)

Catholic Education Council   41 Cromwell Road, London SW7 2DJ (01 584 7491)

Confederation for the Advancement of State Education   81 Rustlings Road, Sheffield S11 7AB (Sheffield 62467)

Council for Educational Advance   c/o Hamilton House, Mabledon Place, London WC1H 9BD (01 387 2442)

Department of Education and Science   York Road, London SE1 (01 928 9222)

Department of Health and Social Security   Alexander Fleming House, Elephant and Castle, London SE1 (01 407 5522)

Home and School Council   81 Rustlings Road, Sheffield S11 7AB (Sheffield 62467)

National Committee for Audio-Visual Aids in Education   33 Queen Anne Street, London W1M 0AL (01 636 5791)

National Foundation for Educational Research in England and Wales   The Mere, Upton Park, Slough, Bucks SL1 2DQ (Slough 28161)

National Froebel Foundation   Froebel Institute, Grove House, Roehampton Lane, London SW15 5PJ (01 878 3489)

National Nursery Examination Board   13 Grosvenor Place, London SW1 (01 235 9961)

National Society for Promoting Religious Education. The,   69 Great Peter Street, London SW1P 2BW (01 222 1672)

National Society of Children's Nurseries   Montgomery Hall, Kennington Oval, London SE11 (01 582 8744)

Nursery School Association of Great Britain and Northern Ireland   89 Stamford Street, London SE1 (01 928 7454)

Pestalozzi Children's Village Trust   Sedlescombe, Battle, Sussex (Sedlescombe 444)

Pre-School Playgroups Association   Alford House, Aveline Street, London SE11 (01 582 8871)

Priority Area Children   32 Trumpington Street, Cambridge CB2 1QY (Cambridge 51456)

Save the Children Fund   29 Queen Anne's Gate, London, SW1 (01 930 2461)

Scottish Office   Whitehall, London SW1 (01 930 6151)

Scottish Office   St. Andrew's House, Edinburgh (031 556 8501)

Service Children's Education Authority   Ministry of Defence, Empress State Building, Fulham, London SW 6 (01 385 1244, Ext. 3528)

Index